Slices of Life
Writing from North America

Thalia Rubio

 Regents/Prentice Hall
Englewood Cliffs, New Jersey 07632

Library of Congress Cataloging-in-Publication Data

Slices of life: writing from North America / [edited by] Thalia
   Rubio.
      p.   cm.
      ISBN 0-13-813296-8
      1. Readers- -North America.   2. North America- -Civilization-
-Problems, exercises, etc.   3. English language- - Textbooks for
foreign speakers.   4. American prose literature.   5. Canadian prose
literature.   6. College readers.   I. Rubio, Thalia, 1951-   .
PE1127.H5S55   1993
428.6'4 - - dc20   92-34184
                                                       CIP

Acquisitions editors: Anne Riddick and Nancy Leonhardt
Managing editor: Sylvia Moore
Production supervision, interior design
          and desktop composition: Noël Vreeland Carter
Desktop production supervision: Molly Pike Riccardi
Electronic scanning: Freddy Flake
Cover design: Mike Fender
Pre-press buyer: Ray Keating
Manufacturing buyer: Lori Bulwin
Scheduler: Leslie Coward

To David,

who only regrets that I didn't include more fishing stories

© 1993 by REGENTS/PRENTICE HALL
A Division of Simon & Schuster, Inc.
Englewood Cliffs, New Jersey 07632

Photo Credits: Page 1, Pierre Pouliot, Quebec Tourist Office; Page 11, Jeff Albertson, Stock, Boston; Page 31, U.P.I.; Page 54, Lionel J. M. Delevigne, Stock, Boston; Page 67, Alan Carey, The Image Works; Page 87, Alan Oddie, PhotoEdit; Page 97, Rhoda Sidney; Page 111, Rhoda Sidney; Page 121, Mimi Forsyth, Monkmeyer Press; Page 133, Erika Stone, Photo Researchers.

Permissions appear on page vi which constitutes a continuation of the Copyright page.

Printed in the United States of America
10 9 8 7 6 5 4 3 2 1

ISBN 0-13-813296-8

Prentice-Hall International (UK) Limited, *London*
Prentice-Hall of Australia Pty. Limited, *Sydney*
Prentice-Hall of Canada Inc. *Toronto*
Prentice-Hall Hispanoamericana, S.A., *Mexico*
Prentice-Hall of India Private Limited, *New Delhi*
Prentice-Hall of Japan, Inc. *Tokyo*
Simon & Schuster Asia Pte. Ltd., *Singapore*
Editora Prentice-Hall do Brasil, Ltda., *Rio de Janeiro*

Contents

Introduction

I'm convinced that ESL students enjoy and appreciate good writing by modern authors. All they need is a boost in understanding the background and the language of a story or essay.

Slices of Life: Writing from North America is a collection of unadapted American and Canadian short stories and essays by well-known authors such as James Thurber, Alice Munro, Grace Paley, and Roch Carrier. (None of these writings is an excerpt from a larger work.) In addition to providing ESL students with practice in reading, writing, and speaking English, this text exposes the reader to good writing by respected modern writers and represents a few of the many points of view in the United States and Canada.

It's happened so often that students ask me questions about how North Americans think and feel, and my answers invariably begin with, "Well, that depends." People outside of North America are often surprised by how heterogeneous the continent is; how we feel depends on where we live, how old we are, and whether we're male or female.

Each person's point of view is also influenced by our race and ethnic group, as well as by economic and educational background. And even then, it's hard to generalize about what we think as Americans and Canadians. It's a big continent, and it would be difficult for one person to describe all North American cultures.

These stories and essays describe different people and regions in North America, as well as themes of interest to students of any nationality. The issues are challenging and open for discussion or writing: justice, old age, discrimination, family relationships. Class discussions and student compositions explore the topics presented in each chapter.

To make these original stories and essays accessible for ESL students, each chapter contains the following:

Before You Begin . . . is a short introduction describing the context and the author. It includes prereading questions that prepare students for major themes of the story or essay.

Footnotes explain words and expressions, as well as historical or cultural references the reader needs in order to understand the story.

Understanding the Story or **Understanding the Essay** checks the student's comprehension by highlighting the major events.

Talking and Writing serves as a guide to class discussion and composition.

More Ideas suggests additional reading and writing, as well as projects that students can do individually or in small groups.

Building Vocabulary contains language exercises that add new words to a student's English vocabulary with each lesson.

For tips on using this book, see **How To Use This Book: Suggestions for the Instructor**, on page vii.

Acknowledgments

Many thanks to Penny Shaw, who encouraged me when this book was just an idea; Hsiao-Ling Koo, Sylvie Blanchin, Susanne Bachinger, and all the others who cheerfully served as my first guinea pigs; Kris Engdahl and Maire Murphy, who reviewed the manuscript; Barbara Bliss, Carol Chandler, and Marsha Watson, who field-tested the book; Mary, Carlos, and Casilda Rubio, who helped with research; and so many people in Boston, San Francisco, Toronto, and Montreal, who told me what they love to read.

Thalia Rubio

Permissions

How to Use This Book
Suggestions for the Instructor

Because each class has its own interests, background, and learning style, and because each teacher has developed a comfortable teaching style, *Slices of Life: Writing from North America* can be used in a variety of ways, depending on the needs of each class.

There are enough stories and essays in this collection for you to select the ones of greatest interest to a particular group of students in a semester course of reading and writing or reading and discussion.

And because this text contains a mixture of story and essay lengths, themes, and reading levels, you can vary the sequence of the chapters and tailor the text to your semester schedule.

Each chapter has open-ended questions for discussion and writing, follow-up reading and writing, and projects outside of class, as well as language exercises.

You might want to cover a chapter in one class, or spend several classes exploring the chapter further. A story or essay might prompt readings from current magazines or newspapers, or additional language exercises to supplement the text.

How to Use "Before You Begin . . ."

Each chapter in this book begins with a section ("Before You Begin") that introduces the author and describes the context of the story or essay.

The suggested prereading questions can be used for a short class discussion before students read the story or essay. These questions encourage students to think about the issues they'll be talking about at the next class. After students have finished the reading, you can further develop some of those ideas.

You might want to help students get a feel for a story or essay's style by having them read the first page silently in class. You can then ask a few questions to be sure that students understand the events, setting, and general mood of what they read. (If a class likes to read out loud, you could have each student read a few sentences.)

One reading strategy you can recommend is to read for meaning the first time, preferably at one sitting. Later, students could read the story or essay again to pick up more vocabulary and further appreciate the writing.

How to Use the Footnotes

Because looking up every new word in the dictionary is distracting and counterproductive, the definitions provided as footnotes focus on the vocabulary students need in order to understand the story or essay. Footnotes also provide background to explain historical or cultural references.

Before students read the story or essay, you can help them become familiar with the vocabulary by highlighting some of the definitions in the footnotes.

Or, after students read the text, you can review some of the vocabulary as a way of checking that students understood the reading.

You can explore different meanings for some of the vocabulary in the text by asking students if they've heard a word before. Students may already be familiar with a word, but they've heard it used to mean something else. Or they might know the vocabulary in another form. For example, they might not know the word *beneficiary*, but they know the word *benefit*.

Another way you can help students build vocabulary is by teaching additional terms or expressions we use when we're discussing the chapter's topic. Students frequently know other words from the same context and are curious about how these different terms are used.

For example, the story "Earthly Justice" includes a few of the words we use to describe what happens in a courtroom, such as *witness* and *jury*. You might want to teach additional vocabulary and expressions in a discussion of how the legal system works: *prosecution, defense, parole, sentence, beyond a reasonable doubt.*

Or you might want to call attention to different forms of the same word, such as *testimony* and *testify*. (You might also want to quiz students on the words that are generated by the class discussion.)

How to Use "Building Vocabulary"

At the end of each chapter are language exercises that emphasize some of the vocabulary presented in the story. You can help reinforce word meanings by giving students the opportunity to use immediately some of the terms they've read.

These vocabulary exercises can be assigned as homework, or the class can be divided into teams or small groups that develop the answers. You could then go over the answers with the class as a whole, exploring different meanings for the words presented, as well as different forms of the words.

Students can also write their own sentences using the vocabulary, either in class or as homework.

How to Use "Understanding the Story"

These comprehension exercises help ensure that students understand the main points of the story or essay before proceeding to the discussion and composition questions.

This section can serve as a warm-up, to get students thinking and talking about the story before going on to the major issues. Or the questions can be assigned as homework to be done when the students read the story.

Students can also work on these exercises in teams or small groups, and then report their answers to the class. (If you have a large class, you could assign specific exercises for each group to work on.)

Another way to have students interpret a story is by retelling it. Students could work in teams developing an oral summary. Or you could divide up the story by pages or by the story's events, assign small groups to summarize the individual sections, and then have the groups present their summaries to the class. Students might want to emphasize the mood and the different points of view in the story, as well as the actions.

How to Use "Talking and Writing"

Because each class is different, the discussion and composition questions on topics in the stories are open-ended. They're designed to prompt additional questions that will allow students to talk or write about their own points of view.

To make a discussion as productive as possible, students can back up their ideas with examples from the story or from their own experiences. (One way to help ensure that everyone in the class participates is to have students work in teams or small groups and then summarize their points of view for the class.)

Any of the questions in "Talking and Writing" can be assigned as a written exercise in class, or as homework. Writing assignments are also included among the projects in the "More Ideas" section in each chapter.

Additional writing topics may be suggested by the story, such as information on using sign language, or what to do in case of an earthquake.

How to Find Resources for "More Ideas"

Now that you've got students interested in the topic, you can encourage them to explore the subject further. The section "More Ideas" in each chapter suggests follow-up reading and writing, and projects that are related to the topics from the class discussion. For example, interviewing people outside class and reporting back to the class is good practice in speaking for students, while providing them with exposure to additional points of view.

If you want to find additional material on a topic presented in a story, and your classes are at a university or high school, check with the school library or administrative office for books, photos, films, speakers, and the names of local organizations.

Because each school's resources are different, the suggested reading list at the end of each chapter is meant to be a place to start rather than a complete reading list. Local newspapers and magazines may have timely information on the subject you're interested in. You can also check the local bookstores, the public library, and the phone book for resources.

You might want to find photos and books describing a story's location, such as Los Angeles, the American Southwest, British Columbia, or Quebec. (Within North America, some tourism offices have toll-free numbers you can call for brochures on specific regions.)

Your specific location can put you at an advantage: For example, if you're near an Indian reservation or a city that has a Canadian Indian or American Indian community, you could contact a local Indian organization and perhaps arrange for a representative to speak to your class. Otherwise, you may need to allow extra time for locating information you're interested in, and call or write to groups outside of your region for material.

If you're not in North America and you want to get more information on an aspect of Canadian or American life, other teachers and language schools may have the material you need. (Bulletin boards can be a convenient way to get information.)

An English-language newspaper or tourist guide may have the names of organizations of North Americans living abroad. You could also contact the Canadian or American consulate for this information.

Your greatest resource may turn out to be your class. Students often have information of interest to the rest of the class, such as personal experiences with deafness. A team of students can call or visit a community association such as an animal-rescue organization, and then bring brochures to share with the other students, or arrange for someone to come to speak to the class.

With a few tips to get them going on a project, students can learn a great deal from doing research and developing their own resources, working individually or in small groups.

A Secret Lost in the Water

Roch Carrier

Translation by Sheila Fischman

Before You Begin . . .

In North America today, it's not unusual for people to move from one region to another, looking for jobs, education, or a better way of life.

It's harder to maintain the old customs when brothers, sisters, cousins, parents and grandparents don't all live nearby. Some traditions get lost, some are changed, some new customs are developed.

In this story, the narrator describes a skill his father taught him when he was a child in rural Quebec, and how that tradition was lost after he left the village he grew up in.

Roch Carrier writes about Quebec, about its traditions and its future. He was born in 1937 in a village southeast of Quebec City.

In the province of Quebec, which includes the cities of Montreal and Quebec City, the majority of the population speaks French as a first language. Because of Canada's history of colonization by both England and France, some people in Canada speak English, some speak French, and some speak both languages.

Carrier's novels, plays, and short stories are well known to both English- and French-speaking readers. The translator, Sheila Fischman, was born in Saskatchewan and has won awards for the quality of her translation. This story is part of Carrier's collection, *The Hockey Sweater and Other Stories*.

Before you read this story, your class could briefly discuss ways in which old traditions end and new traditions begin. How has your society changed in recent years?

A Secret Lost in the Water

Roch Carrier

Translated by Sheila Fischman

After I started going to school my father scarcely talked[1] any more. I was very intoxicated by[2] the new game of spelling; my father had little skill for it (it was my mother who wrote our letters) and was convinced[3] I was no longer interested in hearing him tell of his adventures during the long weeks when he was far away[4] from the house.

One day, however, he said to me: "The time's come to show you something."

He asked me to follow him. I walked behind him, not talking, as we had got in the habit of doing. He stopped in the field before a clump of leafy bushes.

"Those are called alders,"[5] he said.

"I know."

"You have to learn how to choose," my father pointed out.

I didn't understand. He touched each branch[6] of the bush, one at a time, with religious care.

"You have to choose one that's very fine, a perfect one, like this."

I looked; it seemed exactly like the others.

My father opened his pocket knife and cut the branch he'd selected with pious care. He stripped off the leaves and showed me the branch, which formed a perfect Y.[7]

"You see," he said, "the branch has two arms. Now take one in each hand. And squeeze them."

I did as he asked and took in each hand one fork of the Y,[8] which was thinner than a pencil.

"Close your eyes," my father ordered, "and squeeze a little harder . . . Don't open your eyes! Do you feel anything?"

"The branch is moving!" I exclaimed, astonished.[9]

Beneath my clenched[10] fingers the alder was wriggling[11] like a small,

10

20

---

1 **scarcely talked:** talked very little
2 **intoxicated by:** (here) excited about
3 **convinced:** very sure
4 **during the long weeks when he was far away:** while the author's father was traveling on business
5 **alder:** a kind of bush that has a reddish wood. Here, the wood is used as a diving (or dowsing) rod in an old custom of searching for underground water. In this custom, which has a spiritual rather than a scientific basis, the person using the divining rod holds the stick above the ground. If the stick twists and moves to point to a specific place on the ground, the person using the rod begins to dig at that spot for water.
6 **branch:** part of a bush or tree, like an arm
7 **a perfect Y:** exactly the shape of the letter "Y"
8 **one fork of the Y:** one of the two sides of the letter "Y"
9 **astonished:** very surprised
10 **clenched:** tightly held
11 **wriggling:** moving and twisting

3

frightened snake. My father saw that I was about to drop it.

"Hang on[12] to it!"

"The branch is squirming," I repeated. "And I hear something that sounds like
a river!"

"Open your eyes," my father ordered.

I was stunned,[13] as though he'd awakened me while I was dreaming.

"What does it mean?" I asked my father.

"It means that underneath us, right here, there's a little freshwater spring. If
we dig, we could drink from it. I've just taught you how to find a spring.[14] It's
something my own father taught me. It isn't something you learn in school. And
it isn't useless: A man can get along without[15] writing and arithmetic, but he can
never get along without water."

Much later, I discovered that my father was famous in the region because of
what the people called his "gift":[16] Before digging a well[17] they always consulted
him; they would watch him prospecting[18] the fields or the hills, eyes closed, hands
clenched on the fork of an alder bough. Wherever my father stopped, they
marked the ground; there they would dig; and from there water would gush
forth.[19]

Years passed; I went to other schools, saw other countries, I had children, I
wrote some books and my poor[20] father is lying in the earth where so many times
he had found fresh water.

One day someone began to make a film about my village and its inhabitants,
from whom I've stolen so many of the stories that I tell. With the film crew[21] we
went to see a farmer to capture the image[22] of a sad man: His children didn't want
to receive the inheritance[23] he'd spent his whole life preparing for them—the
finest farm in the area. While the technicians were getting cameras and
microphones ready the farmer put his arm around my shoulders, saying:

"I knew your father well."

"Ah! I know. Everybody in the village knows each other . . . . No one feels
like an outsider."[24]

"You know what's under your feet?"

"Hell?" I asked, laughing.

"Under your feet there's a well. Before I dug I called in specialists from the
Department of Agriculture; they did research, they analyzed[25] shovelfuls of dirt;[26]

12 hang on: don't let go
13 stunned: dazed, as though hit in the head
14 spring: (here) source of water that people
can drink
15 get along without: survive without
16 gift: (here) natural ability
17 well: (here) deep hole dug to find water or
oil
18 prospecting: (here) looking for water
19 gush forth: flow suddenly and strongly

20 poor: (here) unfortunate
21 film crew: people who make the movie
22 capture the image: interpret on film
23 receive the inheritance: receive someone's
property after he or she dies
24 outsider: someone who's not part of the
community
25 analyzed: examined scientifically
26 shovelful[s] of dirt: amount of dirt that fits in
a shovel

and they made a report where they said there wasn't any water on my land. With the family, the animals, the crops, I need water. When I saw that those specialists hadn't found any, I thought of your father and I asked him to come over. He didn't want to; I think he was pretty fed up[27] with me because I'd asked those specialists instead of him. But finally he came; he went and cut off a little branch, then he walked around for a while with his eyes shut; he stopped, he listened to something we couldn't hear and then he said to me: 'Dig right here, there's enough water to get your whole flock[28] drunk and drown your specialists besides.'[29] We dug and found water. Fine water that's never heard of pollution."

The film people were ready; they called to me to take my place.   **70**

"I'm gonna show you something," said the farmer, keeping me back. "You wait right here."

He disappeared into a shack which he must have used to store[30] things; then came back with a branch, which he held out to me.

"I never throw nothing away; I kept the alder branch your father cut to find my water. I don't understand, it hasn't dried out."

Moved[31] as I touched the branch, kept out of I don't know what sense of piety[32]—and which really wasn't dry—I had the feeling that my father was watching me over my shoulder; I closed my eyes and, standing above the spring my father had discovered, I waited for the branch to writhe. I hoped the sound of   **80** gushing water would rise to my ears.

The alder stayed motionless in my hands and the water beneath the earth refused to sing.

Somewhere along the roads I'd taken since the village of my childhood I had forgotten my father's knowledge.

"Don't feel sorry," said the man, thinking no doubt of his farm and his childhood; "nowadays fathers can't pass on[33] anything to the next generation."

And he took the alder branch from my hands.

---

27 fed up: impatient
28 flock: group of animals that live or travel together, such as sheep, goats, or birds
29 besides: also
30 store: (here) keep; save

31 moved: (here) emotionally affected
32 piety: religious devotion
33 pass on: (here) give to the next person or persons

Understanding the Story

Work individually or with another student to answer these comprehension questions and review the story's events.

1. When the narrator was a young boy and started school, he and his father didn't talk to each other much because . . .
2. The narrator's father showed his son how to . . .
3. How did the father explain the procedure for finding water? (First, you have to . . .)
4. What happened when the boy squeezed the alder branch?
5. Why did the narrator return to the village where he grew up? Why was the farmer sad?
6. What had the narrator's father done for the farmer years before?
7. What happened when the narrator, as an adult, tried to use the same branch his father had used to help the farmer years before?

Talking and Writing

With your classmates, use these questions as starting points for a discussion of ideas presented in the story. Then select a question and write an essay on the topic.

1. How would you describe the narrator's father? What could he do very well? What couldn't he do? What was his mood when he explained to the farmer where to find water? (Why did the farmer keep the alder branch?)
2. Why do you think the author wrote this story? How do you think he feels about leaving his past behind him?
3. Why do you think the farmer's children don't want the farm? Why would someone move away from the childhood home?
4. What are the advantages and disadvantages of living in a place where everyone knows you?
5. Write a few paragraphs telling something about the customs of your parents, grandparents, or great-grandparents.

    For example, what was different about the culture of your great-grandparents and the time in which they lived? Where did they live and what language did they speak? What kind of work did they do? How did the way they lived reflect events in society, such as war or a changing economy?

6. Write a few paragraphs explaining how your lifestyle is different from the culture you grew up in.

For example, you might have different expectations for how you earn and spend money. You might work in a different kind of job, live in a different part of the country, or speak a different language from the one you heard at home. Are there any modern customs that you think are an improvement over the traditions of the past?

Or write a few paragraphs telling about something in your life that's a continuation of the culture you grew up in. For example, you might celebrate a holiday in the same way that you did as a child.

7. What does the farmer mean at the end of the story? Do you agree? Is there a specific custom in your society that's being lost and you think should be preserved?

How do adults pass on customs to the next generation? If you're a parent, is there a custom you would like to pass on to your children? (Is this easy to do?)

8. Each culture has expressions and sayings to describe its point of view. For example, in English we say, "A bird in the hand is worth two in the bush." What do you think this expression means?

Some of the sayings you'll hear in English include:

- It's the squeaky wheel that gets the grease.
- When in Rome, do as the Romans.
- Don't put all your eggs in one basket.
- Blood is thicker than water.
- If the shoe fits, wear it.
- In the country of the blind, the one-eyed man is king.

Are there sayings in your own language that have the same meanings as some of these expressions?

Write down any proverbs you've heard in English, or expressions you've translated from another language into English, and discuss them with your classmates. Are the meanings obvious?

More Ideas

1. Books and plays by Roch Carrier include *La Guerre, Yes Sir!* and *Floralie, Where Are You?*

Other popular writers from Quebec include Anne Hebert (*The First Garden* and *In the Shadow of the Wind*) and Marie-Claire Blais (*Nights in the Underground* and *A Season in the Life of Emmanuel*).

Stories by different writers from Quebec are translated into English in *Voices from Quebec*, edited by Philip Stratford and Michael Thomas; *Stories from Quebec*, edited by Philip Stratford; and *Invisible Fictions*, edited by Geoff Hancock.

Other collections of Canadian short stories include stories translated from French, as well as stories written in English: for example, *The Penguin Book of Modern Canadian Short Stories*, edited by Wayne Grady; *Best Canadian Short Stories*, edited by John Stevens; and *Great Canadian Short Stories*, selected by Alec Lucas.

2. You and your classmates could develop a reading list of books you recommend. Of the books you like, which ones were written recently? Which ones are older books?

The list should include the author's name, the book's title, and a brief description of the book. (If you're not sure if the book has been translated into English, just provide a rough translation of the book's title.)

3. Interview people outside of class about specific changes in society during their lifetimes. Then write a few paragraphs describing what they said, or report back to the class.

Which new traditions do they like, and which old traditions do they prefer? Which specific changes would they like to see happen in society in the future? For example, how would they change the school system or the public transportation system?

Building Vocabulary

1. You can often get a general idea of a word's meaning by looking at the sentence or paragraph in which it appears.

Take a look at the *italicized* words in the following sentences and guess what each one means. Then check your dictionary to get an exact meaning of each word and see if your guess was correct.

a) When the father taught the son how to prepare an alder branch for use as a divining rod, he first cut the branch from the bush. Then he *stripped off* the leaves.

Stripped off probably means: 1) removed
2) attached

   b) The farmer said he needed water for his family, for the animals, and for the *crops.*

Crops probably means:
1) food he grows
2) food he buys

   c) On his farm, the man went into a *shack* to get the alder branch he'd kept for a long time.

Shack probably means:
1) a small, old building
2) a large, new home

2. Each of the following words from the story has at least two meanings. How is each word used in the story? Check your English-English dictionary for other meanings for these words.

well	moved	intoxicated
spring	gift	poor

3. Using your English-English dictionary, find as many different forms as you can of the following words from the story:

technicians	capture	analyzed

For example, a *technician* is a person using *technical* skills to perform a job in a specific *technology.* (How are these words pronounced?)

Earthly Justice

E. S. Goldman

Before You Begin . . .

We like to think that justice should be applied equally to everyone. But when something happens that involves someone we know or a family member, we may find we have another set of rules for what's fair.

The following story—a mystery—describes a time in a boy's life when he wonders if the ideals he was taught of right and wrong are different for every situation.

Before you read this story, your class could briefly discuss whether or not there is an absolute standard for justice. Are there ever exceptions?

E. S. Goldman was born in 1913 in New York and now lives on Cape Cod, several hours southeast of the city of Boston in the state of Massachusetts.

This author sold his first novel and short story when he was 75. Before his retirement, Goldman was a businessman, the president of an advertising agency, and served in the U. S. Navy.

Note that when you talk or write about this story, you'll be asking, "What if?" (A good opportunity for you to practice using if clauses and the conditional!)

You'll be describing things that aren't true. For example: "If I knew who committed the crime, I would call the police." You'll also be talking or writing about things that could have happened in the past, but didn't happen, such as: "If I had known you were the thief, I would have called the police."

You might find it helpful to read the story twice: once for story meaning, and again to pick up more vocabulary and further appreciate the author's writing.

For practice in learning new words, see the "Building Vocabulary" section at the end of the chapter.

Earthly Justice

E. S. Goldman

At first the words were in the wrong sequence to be heard, for death is slight news unless it carries with it a familiar name. "Killed . . . Pittsburgh . . . *Sherroder!*"

Try it for yourself. How much do you really care about people starving in Africa or sleeping on the sidewalks of Boston or being shot in their garages in Pittsburgh? You care, yes. You're human, and nothing is alien,[1] et cetera. But as if they were your own flesh and blood? No aunt of yours is in any of those fixes[2]— not that you know of. Nothing happens that you care all that much about until you hear a name.

This was 1951 and I was twelve, reading *The Black Arrow* and half listening   **10**
to KDKA on my short wave.[3] I didn't hear anything until I heard the name of my father's sister.

Killed . . . Pittsburgh . . . Sherroder! *Aunt Leora!*

I held on to the book as to a brother in a scary place, while the newscaster put the information in order again for late-arriving minds. (This is the way radio news was managed before jobs were filled by people with no memory of how things should be done. Now newscasters write for radio as if you were tuned from the first word, as if you had nothing to do but sit there and hear them tell the story from A to Z. If you miss the first sentence, with the name of the country where the airplane went down, they never tell you again.)   **20**

"The dead woman's husband, Dr. Myron Sherroder, a well-known Pittsburgh physician, was at home at the time—"

The young don't often play a part[4] as large as being the first to know. I burst out of my room and went down the stairs shouting, "Aunt Leora's been killed! She was shot!"

Leora was very close to us. Not only was she my father's sister but she and my mother had been best friends since middle school. She often came down from Dedham to stay with us at the shore,[5] and after she married and moved to Pittsburgh, the visiting went on as before. Uncle Myron was part of it. The only regret about Myron was that he was a golfer and not a fisherman, as we were in   **30**
our family; but he was accommodating and could be jollied into[6] wading[7] in for smallmouth on a gray day.

---

1 alien: not part of society
2 fix: (here) bad situation
3 short wave: shortwave radio
4 play a part: participate in an important way

5 shore: land along the lake or ocean
6 could be jollied into: could be convinced with jokes
7 wading: walking in very shallow water

Mother was choked and bewildered,[8] and kept saying in an odd, groaning voice I had never heard before, "What do you mean? Leora? What do you mean? What do you mean? Leora?"

She seemed angry with me, which was unreasonable. I had interrupted her sewing—the kind that is done on a small linen drumhead.[9] She thrust out the tambourine, her fingers extended as if to take me by the shoulder to shake out the nonsense, as she had when I was younger. I wasn't sure she would remember the needle. I flinched and looked to Dad.

When my father clenches[10] his jaw, the muscles become bone; his lips bulge as if they have under them the pads a dentist used to slip in to take up saliva.[11] He has never been a slack[12] man in mind or body and does not appreciate slackness in others. He assessed[13] the possibility of error in a twelve-year-old boy.

He held a finger up toward Mother to ask her to hold back, and asked me to say again what I had heard. He went to the phone.

Instead of calling Uncle Myron, as I expected, he asked for Pittsburgh information, and then for the number of the police station nearest the Sherroder address.

The questions he asked the police desk and the way he hung up said enough. Separating the more or less known from the said to be known, the police were able to impart that they had received a report by telephone at 8:17 P.M. from a man who said he was the husband of the deceased.[14] The witness at the scene stated that he had found Mrs. Sherroder on the floor of the garage, apparently dead, apparently as a consequence of multiple wounds, apparently from shotgun fire. The shooting had happened a little more than an hour ago and the investigation was just beginning. Dad made this report piecemeal in a halting[15] voice while he held Mother.

"I'd better call Myron," he said, gently letting her go.

Myron hadn't realized that the news was already on the radio. Detectives[16] were there, taking pictures and asking questions, and he had been waiting for an opportunity to break away and make the call. After they spoke awhile Dad said, "Life is long, Myron. Take every day one at a time. I'll be there on an early plane," and hung up.

Mother had her voice under control. "What did he say?"

"He doesn't know much more than we do. Leora went to an evening meeting of the Handicapped Services Board. He was watching a wildlife documentary on television and didn't hear a thing. When he realized that Leora was late getting

---

8 **bewildered:** confused
9 **linen drumhead:** a piece of cloth stretched tightly like the surface of a drum
10 **clenches:** closes tightly
11 **saliva:** natural liquid in the mouth
12 **slack:** loose

13 **assessed:** evaluated
14 **the deceased:** the dead person (police reports use the word *apparently* to mean that it seems to be true but we're not sure yet)
15 **halting:** hesitating; stopping
16 **detectives:** special police

home, he walked out and saw the garage door open. She was lying beside the car. She was shot. They haven't found a gun." 70

While Mother made the family phone calls, Dad went to the window and stood fully ten minutes with his hands behind his back, staring through the dark at the few stars of houses on the far side of the bay. Mother left Grandma Dewaine for him.[17] He could have waited until morning and seen Grandma on his way to the airport, but he didn't want her to hear the news first from a reporter[18] calling to ask if she had a photograph of her daughter. He told her that Leora had died in an accident, without suffering, and that he would stop by in the morning. Being prepared in this way, she could be relied on to get through the night. Dewaines managed. She was a Dewaine by assimilation.[19]

Mother was also that much a Dewaine, but only that much. She took the 80 phone and asked Grandma if she would like somebody to spend the night with her. She would be glad to come up herself. Would she like Dad to be with her? Would she like her good friend Betty Morse to be called? Mother listened to the timbre[20] of Grandma's voice as she said no, that was unnecessary, she would be all right, and was satisfied. They agreed, as before, that her son would stop there early on his way to the airport.

Although Dad had decided to take the Pittsburgh flight in order to be with Myron on the first difficult day, our family assumed that burial would be in the Dewaine plot[21] in Brewster, on the Cape.[22] When he called to give Myron his flight number, he learned that the burial would be in Pittsburgh. 90

"I don't understand such a decision," Mother said. "Leora has no family in Pittsburgh. They have been married so few years. Myron's family is out west. Your mother is only a two-hour ride from Brewster. Burying Leora in Pittsburgh is inconsiderate.[23] She ought to be in your family plot. Did you say that to him?"

"I made the case.[24] But the decision is Myron's. I can understand that he would want her nearby."

"There are others to think about."

"They have many friends in Pittsburgh."

"Friends are not family. Friends do not come to visit your grave. The decision is a strange one." 100

"It may be arbitrary,[25] but it isn't strange. It's his decision to make. Arguing at a time like this isn't easy."

"When is a good time? After the burial?" I seldom heard Mother that sharp with Dad.

17 left Grandma Dewaine for him: let him call Grandma Dewaine
18 reporter: someone who reports the news for radio, television, or a newspaper
19 was a Dewaine by assimilation: had become a Dewaine from spending time with Dewaines
20 timbre: mood
21 Dewaine plot: section of the cemetery for the Dewaine family
22 the Cape: Cape Cod in the state of Massachusetts
23 inconsiderate: not thinking of someone else's needs
24 made the case: presented the argument
25 arbitrary: for no specific reason

"He and Leora chose the site with care. In his view, he is accommodating her wishes."

"In his view."[26]

We all went to Pittsburgh for the funeral.

When people have lived their years, it is possible to take satisfaction in memory, and even possible for levity to soften grief, and after long illness it is possible to speak of relief, but this was a day of harsh, unrelieved mourning,[27] the most solemn[28] day of my life. In the chapel Uncle Myron sat between his brother, Andrew, and my father, and beside Father was Grandma Dewaine. Then Uncle Tom Dewaine, then Mother. They sat by bloodline.[29] Except around a dinner table I had never before, at an occasion, seen Father not sit beside Mother. Because of the nature of the wound the casket was closed.

Very little was said among us. When Grandma shook with hidden sobs, Dad took her hand. I did the same to my sister, Marnie, at first awkwardly, and then, when she clutched it to show how glad she was to have it, with (I suppose the right word is) pride.

After the cemetery Mother took Marnie and me directly to the plane. She did not want to stay over. She said tomorrow was a school day and we should be back. My father spent the rest of the day in Pittsburgh with Myron, talking to the police and the district attorney. They posted a reward.[30]

You may have forgotten the story by now, or may have it confused with the celebrated case of the Cleveland doctor's wife. The death of Leora Dewaine Sherroder was much less noteworthy than the Cleveland story, but it was closely followed in Pittsburgh and on Cape Cod, where the phone book includes three columns of Dewaines. You call a Dewaine to put on a roof, survey your land, pick up your rubbish, send you a nurse. To fish out of Rock Harbor you sign on the *Cape Corsair*, Cap'n Pres Dewaine. You bank with Len at Samoset 5¢ Savings. To cater a wedding you call Carolyn. Dewaines hidden by marriage under other names must fill many columns more. The only big rich Dewaines I know of are the Ananders, through Cousin Peg. Delbert Anander knew what land to buy and how long to hold it, and how to run a bank and when to sell it. My father was the fourth Dewaine with the hardware and heating store, the first with the oil trucks.

The story in the newspaper about the will[31] gave me an uncomfortable feeling that others might not see Aunt Leora's death as I did. It didn't say anything that wasn't already known in the family: except for named bequests, everything was left to Uncle Myron as remainderman. They had no children. Simply stating in

---

26 **in his view:** from his point of view
27 **mourning:** sadness over personal loss, such as when someone dies
28 **solemn:** serious
29 **by bloodline:** according to membership in the family

30 **posted a reward:** offered an amount of money
31 **will:** (here) legal document a person writes that determines who owns the property after he or she dies

the newspaper that Myron was Leora Dewaine's heir[32] seemed to imply[33] something.

In follow-up stories Leora became the heiress of the Dewaine fortune, the Dewaines became Mayflower[34] descendants. The family had oil interests. A reporter discovered that a brother of Leora's great-grandfather had been a governor of Massachusetts; the family became politically influential.[35] Myron was a kidney specialist, he had been consulted by a Mellon. He was a member of a country club; he became a socialite doctor. They had no children. The socialite[36] doctor was the sole heir.

With such people, in such an environment, all things are possible. You don't have to go beyond your own mind.   150

Uncle Myron was my friend, who took me to the zoo, and to the museum to see the dinosaurus xylophony[37] stretching down the hall (From "*zonnnq*" on his nose—Myron had impressive range—to "*tinnnggg*"), and to Forbes Field to see a big-league baseball game.

We sat in a box behind first base. A high foul[38] went up, and I saw that if it did not go up forever, it would come down sometime later that day right where I was. Everybody around me stood up. I thought if I could get my hands on that ball I could hold it.

The day was chilly, and the men wore gloves, but I was a boy and of course   160 hadn't thought I needed gloves. While my head followed the nearly vertical rise of the ball Uncle Myron grasped my left hand. "Here's a glove to take the sting out." He raised his voice to the crowd around us. "Give the kid a shot at it."[39]

They cleared a space. I don't think any crowd today would stand back to give a kid a shot. I followed the ball higher than I had ever seen a ball go, while I worked the bunching out of the palm of Uncle Myron's glove and displayed the floppy fingers as a target.

I was sure I was under it, but misjudged the angle of the fall, backed into the men, and finally fell backward into the seats. The ball, ignoring the chance to make a stylish landing in a gray suede glove, dropped beyond my farthest reach.   170 My failure that day—despite the cooperation of the entire world to help me succeed—is not yet forgotten. It enhances the memory of Myron Sherroder, my friend, who the newspaper said, without saying it, might have been the one who killed Aunt Leora.

---

32 heir: person who gets the property when someone dies
33 imply: say something indirectly
34 Mayflower: boat used by the Pilgrims, landing in 1620 in Plymouth on Cape Cod. The Pilgrims were the settlers of the first colony in New England.
35 politically influential: knows people in government

36 socialite: someone who's active in wealthy society
37 dinosaurus xylophony: dinosaurs were huge animals that lived millions of years ago
38 high foul: in baseball, a ball that's hit high in the air and comes down outside the area where the game is played
39 shot: (here) try

I began then to understand how words say things that aren't in them. Words reach for meanings that are already inside the hearer. In a card trick the magician fans out the cards and says, "Pick one." Psych the cards as hard as you want,[40] you can't psych a ten of diamonds out of a tarot deck. You have to take a card that's there. I wanted it another way, but the statement that the husband of the
180   murdered woman was the beneficiary[41] of her will picked up the card from my standard human deck.[42]

I began then to read about the case as others would. One day at school I took a question from a friend—"How is your uncle coming with that murder case?" It said to me that when they spoke of Leora Sherroder's murder in their home, they assumed that her husband, the socialite doctor who had inherited her money, was probably involved in some way. And I could not help thinking it too.

I was troubled. I didn't tell my father how I felt, but I put a question in a form that betrayed me.[43] "What if—?"

Before responding, my father laid his narrow eyes on me. "That's the way
190   people are. In this house we do not think like that. My sister was a good judge of character. She chose your Uncle Myron. As far as we know[44] they had a good marriage."

Why "As far as we know . . ."?

I never heard my father say anything about innocence. What I understood him to say was that we had to wait respectfully, withholding judgment, as long as the process took—forever, if necessary. We had a stake[45] in the values of organized society.

We were right to wait. In a few weeks the Pittsburgh police let it out[46] that they were looking for a white man about forty years old, with a butch haircut,[47]
200   driving a late-model Plymouth white two-door. He had been seen several times in the neighborhood in the week of the murder and nobody knew who he was. They found what they believed was the gun, in the Allegheny River about five miles from the house, and began to trace[48] it. The gun was a Winchester twelve-gauge. A lot of them are around. We have one in our house.

That got the newspapers going again.

Dad went to Pittsburgh. He saw Uncle Myron. He talked to the district attorney and to Detective Gertner, who had had the case from the beginning. Gertner said privately that they weren't getting anywhere looking for the man in the Plymouth. No fingerprints were found on the gun; they hadn't been able to
210   trace it.

40 psych the cards as hard as you want: (slang) concentrate on the cards to try to influence them
41 beneficiary: person who gets the property when someone dies
42 deck: (here) all the playing cards together
43 betrayed me: indicated my true feelings

44 as far as we know: according to the information we have
45 stake: (here) interest; investment
46 let it out: (here) indirectly told people
47 butch haircut: very short haircut
48 trace: (here) find the original owner

The detective told my father something else. Dad did not look at Mother as he reported it.

"They are talking to a woman they say Myron had been seeing before—" It's not easy to say *Before my sister was murdered.* "I have to say that bothers me."

"What did Myron say to that?" Mother asked.

"He's where he was. He knows they're looking into a lot of things."

"Did he say he knew what they were looking into?"

"He mentioned the gun and the man who had been seen in the neighborhood."

"That's all been in the papers. He didn't say anything about the woman?"

"He said, 'And the usual gossip you can expect.'"   220

"Did he say what that was?"

"No, and I didn't ask him. He is a smart man. He can guess what comes to me."

That conversation reinforced my impression that Myron was guilty. I was not so persuaded that I would have been unable to be a fair juror; but I thought Myron was probably the killer, and I was sure I was not the only person in our house to think it—not since Father's "As far as we know . . . ," not since Mother's refusal to stay in Pittsburgh after the funeral, and the clipped severity of her manner when Myron's name came up.

Uncle Myron was indicted for first-degree homicide.[49] I didn't know why the   230 language needed another word for murder.

"That must mean he's pretty[50] guilty,"[51] I said.

Expressing judgment in an important matter made me feel important. I didn't know that before the law you are either guilty or not; "pretty" has nothing to do with it.

My father stiffened his lips. "I don't want that said again in my hearing. A trial is to find that out. The adversarial system[52] we have in this country is the best way to get at the truth. Each side puts up the best argument it knows how. You may think you know Uncle Myron's defense, but you don't till you hear it argued. I don't want you to forget that."   240

Dad went to the trial to hear the woman for himself, for the two days she was a witness. She testified that she had carried the gun from the garage when Uncle Myron told her to and had thrown it in the river. Uncle Myron's lawyer suggested that she was seeking revenge because Myron had started to see other women. He brought out that she was an alcoholic. She and a former boyfriend were involved

49 indicted for first-degree homicide: officially accused of murder
50 pretty: (here) enough
51 guilty: not innocent. In the United States and Canada, a person is considered innocent until proven guilty in a court of law. It's the responsibility of the prosecution to prove that the accused person is guilty. This is one way the justice system is kept fair.
For a person to be convicted of a crime, the evidence must show "beyond a reasonable doubt" that the accused person is guilty.
A case might be tried before a judge alone or before a jury of twelve citizens from the community. Before a jury can deliver a verdict of guilt or innocence, everyone on the jury must agree. Otherwise, the trial is a "mistrial."
52 adversarial system: a system in which two sides present opposing arguments

in a larceny,[53] and the district attorney had made a deal to let her off a perjury[54] charge in exchange for her testimony[55] in the Sherroder case. She could even have been the one who committed the murder. Myron's lawyer brought all that out.

"She didn't make a very good witness," my father said. "Myron's lawyer
250 doesn't think she will be convincing to the jury."

But no one doubted that Myron had something going with her—she knew too much about his life.

Myron said she knew only enough to make up the rest in order to get the reward. "I'm sorry all this comes out in this way, which must seem sordid to you," he said to my father. "I can't blame you for what you must think."

"Of course he can't blame you," Mother said to my father. "What are you supposed to think? Leora was your sister. Did he still pretend he hadn't been going out with other women?"

"He said he had done what a lot of men do, and he apologized for it. He said
260 Leora would have understood why he saw other women if she had known, even if she might not necessarily have condoned it."[56]

"'Not necessarily.' I should think."

Myron had said, "I am not asking you to tell me what you now think about this. I only want you to hear me when I say I had nothing to do with Leora's murder. I am entirely innocent."

"What *do* you think?" Mother asked.

My father's jaw muscles became bone. "I wasn't hired to be God," he said.

The afternoon the case went to the jury, deliberations[57] weren't expected to start until the next day. I was in bed with the lights out and the radio to my ear
270 when a bulletin came on that the jurors had decided to convene[58] to test their sentiment. They found they had a verdict[59] right away. The judge was coming in to hear it.

I got up and told Mother and Dad. We sat in the library and waited.

None of us made a guess what the verdict would be. It wasn't a ballgame, or somebody else's family, or anything that doesn't count, where you can show how smart or how dumb you are. When something is close to you, you don't look at it the way you do if you're separated from it. In traffic the car ahead of you can be in the middle and won't get out of the way and you get mad. When you're in position to go around, you see the driver is somebody you know well and you
280 cool off. You wave. Anything that is close to you is different.

The verdict was not guilty.

---

53 larceny: stealing
54 perjury: lying while testifying in court, after promising to tell the truth
55 testimony: speech given by a witness in court

56 condoned: forgiven; accepted
57 deliberations: discussions by the jury before deciding on guilt or innocence
58 convene: have a meeting
59 verdict: decision of guilty or not guilty

To tell the truth, I didn't feel the relief I had expected from knowing that my uncle wouldn't have to spend the rest of his life in jail. I certainly wouldn't have taken any joy in a guilty verdict, but it would have been more fitting and satisfying to human nature.

I suppose I am saying that my Aunt Leora, of my father's blood and therefore of mine, had been murdered, and that the way we are made requires that somebody be accountable.[60] Almost any somebody, rather than nobody. I'm the first to agree that for the sake of civilization we must respect the verdict of a court; still, that verdict isn't necessarily satisfactory to our natural sense of what **290** is just.

I sensed that my mother felt the same way, and for a moment that my father did too, but he said abruptly, "That's the verdict. The reward stands.[61] We are going to look that much harder."

He called Uncle Myron and told him that he knew the experience had been hard but he hoped Myron could get on with his life. He invited him down to do some fishing. They arranged a weekend. Mother said, "You invited him *here*? I would just as soon you hadn't."[62]

"I don't want to lose touch."

"I will never be comfortable with Myron. But it's up to you. I suppose men **300** understand these things better." I supposed that wasn't what she thought.

Uncle Myron was grateful that we made him one of us. The truth is that without Leora he was a foreign substance. He could not attach himself by shaking my hand and telling me I had grown an inch a week; by swinging my sister in the air; by trying to find a place to kiss on Mother's averted cheek. Dad hurried him through the greetings and got him to the stairs leading to the tower room overlooking the bay. He and Leora had always had that room.

Next day was raw and drizzly,[63] an ordinary April day. A good breeze came across from the northeast, and the tide went out all morning. It wouldn't be very comfortable on the open bay. I thought they would fish Drum Pond, but Dad said, **310** "Myron, have you ever fished Shelf Lake with me?" Uncle Myron couldn't remember that he had.

I don't think Myron ever fished before he married Leora. As often as not when they visited, he would go over and play the Great Dune course while the rest of us went to a bass pond. Dad certainly wasn't going to play golf and he didn't offer any choices.

"We'll go over there. We'll get some shelter from the wind. I have a new suit of Red Ball waders you can break in for me. I'll wear my old one."

They loaded rods, boots,[64] waders,[65] parkas, slickers, boxes of lures, leaders,

---

60 accountable: responsible
61 stands: (here) is still offered
62 would just as soon you hadn't: wish you hadn't

63 raw and drizzly: cold and rainy
64 rods, boots . . . : things needed for fishing
65 waders: special boots for walking in low water

320 spare lines, and tools, and a lunch. They were ready for bass or trout all day in any weather. They dropped me at Everbloom Nursery,[66] where I had a Saturday-morning job.

Bob Everbloom and I were moving azaleas from the back field to front beds, beginning in a drizzle we knew would get heavier. When it did, Bob decided we had had enough of outside work. I could have worked under glass, but I didn't come to do that. I liked to be outside on weekends. I said I would skip it, they didn't need me in the greenhouse. I borrowed Bob's bike[67] and headed for Shelf Lake. My father and Myron were carrying enough extra tackle to outfit me.

All this country around here, all of Cape Cod, consists of the tailings left after
330 the great glacier[68] thawed and backed off to Canada. It's all rock brought down by the ice and melted out, sand, and a skin of topsoil from decay. Those big stands of trees are in sand not too far down. The only clay is wherever you happen to dig your foundation; you can't get drainage.

After the margin sand Shelf Lake is a basin of underwater boulders fed by the runoff from Sparks' Hill. The surrounding land is in conservation.[69] What falls they let lie. The bones of old downed trees lie around the rim. Those spines of big fish stuck in the ground are dead cedars. A couple of paths lead in through heavy woods.

It was too raw a day for people to come for wilderness walks, and most of the
340 fishermen around here either are commercial and need the quantities they get in salt water or want the fast action of bay fishing. Our Jeep was the only vehicle parked at NO VEHICLES PERMITTED BEYOND THIS SIGN. On a busy day as many as two might be there. I locked the bike to the Jeep's bumper and went down the woods path.

Nearing the bottom, I heard my father call, "Left, farther left, toward the cove."

Through the trees I saw that they were both in hip-deep, Uncle Myron a hundred or so yards west and working farther. Rain dimpled the water. Away from the lee of the hill, fans of wind patterned the surface like shoaling fish. I was
350 troubled by something but didn't concentrate on what it might be, because I was busy picking through catbrier that snatched into the path.

"Another ten yards. They're in there," my father called out.

Then I realized what troubled me. Myron was on the edge of the shelf[70] that gave the lake its name. It fell off without any warning into a deep hole. I took a running step and opened my mouth to shout, but before I could, he let out a bellow[71] and pitched down.

---

66 **nursery:** (here) a business that grows and sell flowers
67 **bike:** bicycle
68 **great glacier:** great mass of ice that covered the region long ago

69 **in conservation:** protected in the natural condition
70 **shelf:** flat horizontal surface, such as a bookshelf
71 **bellow:** yell

My mind churned[72] with what could be done and what I had to do. I could get around to the shoreline nearer to him, and dive in and help him out of his gear.[73] I could—

But I didn't move, because, more dumbfounding[74] to me than the accident   **360** itself, my father acted as though it weren't happening. He heard Myron and saw him flail to stay afloat and go under in seconds. He knew as I did that Myron, under the roiled water, would be fighting to get out of his parka and sweater, then out of the waders that were filling and turning into anchors;[75] but my father turned away and cast.[76]

I couldn't stop staring at him. Dad began to reel in.[77] His rod bent. He had a bass fighting and flopping like a sandfilled stocking. Working light tackle,[78] he had to give and take carefully not to lose it. The ripples settled out of the water where Myron had been, and my father was unslipping the net with his free hand and playing the bass with the other.   **370**

I was terrified—not frightened, terrified—as much for my father as for myself. He had deliberately led my uncle to be drowned. I tried to make the events happen differently in my mind, but I could not doubt what I had seen and heard.

When at last I found the will[79] to move, I moved not toward him but back up the trail, to be away and alone long enough to get my bearings[80] before I had to face him.

I rode the bike in the rain to the nursery and put it in the tool shed. Nobody was around. I didn't have to talk to anybody.

Behind the mall,[81] down the road from Everbloom's, the receiving platforms[82]   **380** stood on iron legs, backed against the cement block, the cheap side of the stores. Weather swept over the blacktop,[83] pooling where the graders hadn't got it right. On raw bulldozed ground beyond the blacktop, weeds and a few stringy locusts tried to start a forest again. A tree line the bulldozers wouldn't get to for a few years drifted into the mist at the end of this world. Nobody ever came back there unless a truck was unloading. I hunched under a dock.

As the evidence against Uncle Myron had become stronger and weaker and stronger again in the year that had passed since Aunt Leora's death, I had felt in myself many times a certainty that he had killed her sufficient to imagine myself doing to him as my father had.   **390**

I had imagined aiming the gun—the same gun, the twelve-gauge, to make the justice more shapely—and firing. I could do that, I had told myself.

---

72 churned: turned violently
73 gear: (here) fishing equipment
74 dumbfounding: confusing
75 anchors: heavy objects thrown into the water to keep a ship from moving
76 cast: (here) threw the line on his fishing rod out into the water
77 reel in: pulled in the line on his fishing rod

78 light tackle: fishing line that isn't strong
79 will: (here) motivation, strength
80 get my bearings: organize my thoughts
81 mall: shopping center
82 receiving platforms: areas in back of stores where trucks unload goods for the stores to sell
83 blacktop: surface of the road

Under the shelter of the platform I knew I had only been telling myself a story. I could have put my finger on the trigger[84] but not pulled. I might have led him to step off the shelf, but duty as I understood it, as I had learned it from my father, would have compelled me to save a drowning man even if I had been the one who put him in peril.[85]

I had had the chance and not used it. I had not burst out of the trees shouting. I had not waded in. I had watched, and then run to get the bike.

400   My father had pulled the trigger and turned away as if it were nothing.

I drowned in questions. Why had I done nothing? Was it because I was young and not much was expected of me? Was it because it had happened in the presence of my father, and it was not my place to put myself forward where he did not? Was I bound[86] to silence forever? What would happen if he were suspected? And stories were in the paper?

And he went on trial?

Would I come forward to witness for him, to give an account of the event that matched whatever his was? Would I be able to stick with a lie like that—for my father, who had made lying a hard thing for me to do?

410   What if somebody in one of the cars that had passed on the road recognized me? What if I was reported, and taken to the police station and asked what I knew and why I had not volunteered it before?

What was expected of me? I had nobody to ask.

The rain drew off. I would have to go home. I took with me the simplest of stories to account for myself. I had biked to Nickerson Park, in the direction of Shelf Lake, and when the rain began had got under the cover of a firewood shed.

A diver found Uncle Myron bundled at the foot of the shelf in forty feet of water. My father explained that Myron had been warned, that he must have lost track of where he was while my father had been inattentive. Anybody who knew
420 that water and how you could become engrossed[87] working a five-pound bass on a three-pound line understood how easily it could happen.

Myron's brother came to the Cape to make arrangements to ship the body to Pittsburgh for burial alongside Aunt Leora. He was Uncle Andrew to me, although we never knew that family very well. They were westerners, we were easterners; we met only at anniversary parties, weddings, funerals.

He said Myron had been a good brother and he would miss him. I suppose in some way he felt that my father had a degree of responsibility, since the accident had happened in our territory, so to speak, but he didn't indicate it.

The circumstances were such that the card of suspicion never turned over in
430 anybody's head. Nobody who knew Ben Dewaine would have thought it for an instant.

I lived difficult years with my father after that, although all the difficulties

---

84 trigger: part of the gun that is pulled to make the gun fire

85 peril: danger
86 bound: (here) obligated; tied
87 engrossed: thinking very hard

were within me. On the surface our close relationship was undisturbed. We fished and hunted together as before, and I took many problems to him for a viewpoint.

Since I had declared against going into the family business, my parents thought that I might become a lawyer. I have an orderly mind and some ability to express myself, and therefore I thought so too. I was well along in college before I decided to do other work. In those early years, the years in which we allow ourselves to think abstractly, I often reflected about justice, but I never allowed myself to discuss it with my father, fearing that one word would take me to **440** another until I reached one that I would regret.

I came to have considerable respect for Pilate.[88] I thought how much more difficult Pilate's problem may have been than the press reported. I would want to know more about what kind of man Pilate was before I concluded that he had a worn-out conscience or that he had settled for an epigram.[89]

Nine years later the man with the brush haircut turned himself in.[90]

He couldn't live with it. It happens all the time. They see the victim's face at night and think of what a life is and what it is to destroy one, and they get disgusted with themselves. They begin to think there may be eternal judgment[91] after all, and they will be accountable. They show up at police stations and have **450** to convince desk officers that they aren't nuts.[92] They call up reporters and meet them in diners. They ask priests to be go-betweens. They hire lawyers to get them the best deal.

The man's name was Rome Hurdicke.

Again it was a story in the papers. He had parked, looking for opportunity as he had on other nights, and this night a dark place beside the lane beyond the Sherroder house had been the cover that attracted him. He had followed Aunt Leora into the garage intending to bluff her with the gun.[93] She had been slow to respond. He thought she was about to call for help. He panicked[94] and shot her and then thought only about getting away. The most singular event in two lives, **460** and it was from beginning to end so ordinary that it could have been set in type like a slogan to be called up with a keystroke.

The newspapers rehashed[95] it and noted the strange fate that had befallen so many people associated with the crime. Four of the jurors were dead. The judge had been killed in a private-plane accident. The woman who had claimed to be the well-known socialite doctor's mistress had committed suicide. The husband of the murdered heiress had drowned in a fishing accident on Cape Cod.

Hurdicke was undoubtedly the man. He told the police where and when he

88 Pilate: government official of ancient Rome who heard the case against Jesus, the founder of Christianity
89 epigram: a kind of saying. (Pilate is quoted as saying "I wash my hands of it.")
90 turned himself in: gave himself up to the police
91 eternal judgment: punishment or reward after death
92 nuts: (slang) crazy
93 bluff her with a gun: use a gun to pretend he was going to hurt her
94 panicked: suddenly got frightened and lost control
95 rehashed: went over the same information again

had bought the gun, and they verified the numbers. They found the Plymouth still
470 in service, three owners forward and a coat of white paint two coats down. It was
an old case, and because he had turned himself in, he got twenty years and was
eligible for parole[96] in twelve.

And so Uncle Myron's life had been taken without cause.[97]

I think somebody—perhaps his brother, Andrew—may care for Myron as we
cared for Aunt Leora, and if he knew the circumstances of his death would yearn
for human justice as my father did. I don't know. I can't deal with[98] how Uncle
Andrew might feel. My father is my flesh and blood, and he is a good man.

I can't deal with my own guilt. If I had responded on the instant that I saw
Uncle Myron pitch into the water, could I have saved him?

480 I don't know. I will never get over not making the attempt, but confession[99]
offers me no way out, for it would be to witness against my father. I am tribal
enough to say that my duty is to him, to keep the secret. In some matters what is
not known does not exist.

After Hurdicke confessed, I watched my father closely. I trembled that he
might turn himself in or even take his own life in remorse.[100] I didn't know if he
would be more likely to do it if he knew that I knew his secret. Did he think that
he alone knew what had happened at Shelf Lake? As a son who had become also
a father, I knew that some parts of his life he intended to be an object lesson for
me, but I couldn't be certain which.

490 His manner, naturally reserved, became wintry. He gave up his places on
church and hospital boards, and reduced his responsibilities at the company. Time
passing without incident did not lull me into supposing that he had made his
peace with Uncle Myron's ghost, any more than Hurdicke had made his with
Aunt Leora's. Nevertheless, he went on with his life in a normal, though
increasingly subdued,[101] way, into his retirement years.

He entered then a remission in which he seems to have regained his appetite
for a more active life. Mother said the other day, "He had a new garden turned
over. He is talking about going west in the fall to hunt ram. He rejoined his skeet
club. I think he is coming into good years."

500 That may be, but I have marked my calendar.

I don't know how Father accepts that the man who shot his sister in the face
with a twelve-gauge Winchester has been paroled. Hurdicke will be released next
week. I can only hope that my father has had enough of dealing out justice on
earth.

---

96 eligible for parole: could be released early from prison
97 without cause: for no reason
98 can't deal with: (slang) can't think about; can't get involved with

99 confession: admission of guilt
100 remorse: guilt and sorrow over what he'd done
101 subdued: quiet

Understanding the Story

Work individually or with another student to answer these comprehension questions and review the story's events.

1. The narrator was listening to the radio and didn't hear anything until he heard the name of _____.

2. After the news of the murder, the narrator's father didn't call Uncle Myron first. Instead, he called _____

    _____.

3. Myron said he was _____ when his wife was killed.

Mark the following sentences true or false. If the sentence is false, correct it. If it's true, explain further.

4. ___ The narrator's mother was upset because Leora would be buried in Pittsburgh.

5. ___ Very few people with the last name *Dewaine* live on Cape Cod.

6. ___ Myron got no money when Leora died.

Refer to the story for the answers to the following questions:

7. Describe what happened at the ball park.

8. Describe the man the police were looking for.

9. a) Who confessed to the murder of Leora?

    b) Were you surprised to find out who the criminal was?

10. a) Why did the murderer confess?

    b) Why did he do it?

    c) What is the evidence against him?

Talking and Writing

With your classmates, use these questions as starting points for a discussion of ideas presented in the story. Then select a question and write an essay on the topic.

1. What did the boy's father do at Shelf Lake? Was his action justified?

Would the father's action have been justified if he'd seen Myron commit the crime, but the jury found Myron innocent? What if the father thought he saw Myron commit the crime but the father was wrong?

2. How do you imagine the father feels now? What do you think will happen next? (What does the last line of the story mean?)

3. Imagine you are the son in this story and the father has been accused of murder. What would you say at his trial? What would be the father's defense?

    What kind of person is the father, according to the son? How does the son feel about his father? Why was he frightened for his father when he saw what happened to Myron?

4. Is this a believable story? Why or why not? How does the author show the boy's confusion about the right thing to do? How does the author emphasize the importance of family?

5. Does the narrator think the definition of justice is different if you know the people involved? What do you think? (Are the family's needs more important than society's needs?)

    Are there times when it's all right to take the law into your own hands? Give examples. If we feel the legal system isn't doing its job, is it all right for someone else to administer justice?

6. Why didn't the boy help Myron at Shelf Lake? Do you think his action was right or wrong? If you were the narrator, what would you do now?

    Would the son's action have been as easy to understand if he had actively helped the father in taking revenge on Myron? What if the son thought Myron was innocent? (What if the government asked the son to help kill someone?)

7. Imagine you're Myron. How does it feel to have people think you might be guilty? Retell the story in a few paragraphs from Myron's point of view. Why did the narrator's family think Myron might be guilty?

    What does the narrator explain about human nature, and about the nature of words, that made him believe Myron might be guilty? How did the narrator feel after Myron is found innocent? (Why did the narrator want someone to be found guilty?)

More Ideas

1. Spend a few minutes practicing a courtroom trial scene and then present it to the class. You'll need a judge, two lawyers, a

defendant, and a crime. You could also have a few people serve as a jury.

For example, the defendant could be accused of stealing a car, or having a dog that barks constantly, or giving a noisy all-night party. (If you have a video, you could tape the trial.)

You might want to visit a local courthouse to see a real trial going on. (Most trials in North America are open to the public.) You could write a few paragraphs describing a courtroom scene, using some of the vocabulary from this story.

2. Find a newspaper story that describes a crime or a courtroom trial. Write a paper about the case, or summarize the story for the class.

3. Do you think we assume a person is guilty if he or she is accused of a crime? What do you think could be done to be sure the accused person is not considered guilty until the government has proven its case?

For example, we say a case is "tried by the media" to mean that the newspapers and television had already decided someone's guilt or innocence before the jury did. (Have any cases like this been in the news recently?)

Should newspapers not be allowed to report what is happening in a trial? Or is it the public's right to know what is happening in the courtroom?

4. Capital punishment is legal in some states in the United States today. Do you think the death penalty is fair? (What if the person is later found to be innocent?)

Write a short letter to the newspaper or to someone in the government expressing support or opposition to the death penalty. Give reasons to support your opinion.

5. What qualities do you need to be a good lawyer, a good judge, or a good juror? What makes a good police officer?

Do you know someone who is a lawyer, a judge, a police officer, or has been on a jury? You could interview that person and report back to the class. For example, you could ask if movies and television programs that describe the legal system are accurate.

6. Libraries and bookstores near you will have many mysteries, detective stories, and crime stories. We sometimes refer to crime stories as "whodunits" (who "done" it?).

Suggested reading: *The Maltese Falcon* by Dashiell Hammett; *The Big Sleep* by Raymond Chandler; *Double Indemnity* by James Cain; and *A Woman's Eye*, edited by Sarah Paretsky; *Fingerprints: A Collection of Mystery Stories by Crime Writers of Canada*, edited by Beverley Beetham-Endersby. A Canadian mystery writer is Howard Engel: *Murder on Location.*

Scoundrel Time by Lillian Hellman describes justice during the McCarthy era in the United States. *Brothers and Keepers* by John Wideman describes life in prison. A story about revenge in 19th century America is *Moby Dick* by Herman Melville. (*Moby Dick* was also made into a movie, starring Gregory Peck.)

7. Write a few paragraphs of your own mystery. You could begin the story with: "It was a dark and stormy night."

   Or you could write a summary of one of your favorite mysteries.

Building Vocabulary

1. Each of the following words from the story has at least two meanings. How is each word used in the story?

   Check your dictionary for other meanings for these words. You might want to work with a partner or in small groups; each group could have two or three words to look up and then report back to the class.

alien	bluff	will	fix
deck	shot	trace	pretty
stand	gear	cast	tackle
bearings	bound	turn in	nursery

2. Using your English-English dictionary, write other forms of the following words from the story. For example, if the word is a noun, write the adjective. Write as many forms as you can.

heir	imply	betrayed	panicked

The Convert

Lerone Bennett, Jr.

Before You Begin . . .

An important part of American history is the civil rights movement of the 1950s and 1960s, when African-Americans in the United States risked their lives trying to gain their rights as Americans to work, live, and travel freely.

The following story takes place in Mississippi, in the part of the United States we call the deep South, where extensive segregation laws determined where African-Americans could go and what they could do.

This doesn't mean that there has been equality for African-Americans in the northern states. In many ways, discrimination against African-Americans in the North has simply been less obvious than the racism in the southern states.

But the story of the civil rights movement takes place in the South because that's where segregation was required by law, and that's where people were killed because of those laws.

Segregation laws specified that African-Americans couldn't have access to most of society's services, or were only allowed to use them in a limited way. For example, African-Americans had to attend separate schools that were of poorer quality than those attended by whites. Theaters, public parks, and playgrounds were either closed to African-Americans, or had separate areas for "colored."

Restaurants and hotels often refused service to people who weren't white. Segregation laws prevented African-Americans from using public libraries, museums, and swimming pools. When the nearest hospital was for whites only, many people who needed immediate medical attention died before they could get help.

These segregation laws were strictly and violently enforced. In this story, a man puts himself in a dangerous position when he challenges the "Jim Crow" laws that required African-Americans to sit in separate cars when traveling on a train, and wait for trains in separate waiting rooms.

Lerone Bennett, Jr. was born in Mississippi in 1928 and now lives in Chicago, where he is senior editor for *Ebony* magazine. His writing on the experiences of African-Americans includes a biography of Martin Luther King, Jr. and books on African-American history—as well as articles, short stories, and poems.

Before you read this story, your class could discuss people who struggled to achieve their freedom. What methods did they use? Were they successful?

Of all the people who came to live in the United States in the eighteenth and nineteenth centuries, only the Africans were forced to come as slaves.

Thrown into ships in west Africa, many Africans did not live to see America. Those who survived the journey often watched their families divided as each member was sold to a slave owner in the United States.

By the early 1800s, slavery was legal only in the southern part of the United States, where the economy depended on agriculture—especially the growing of cotton—and large numbers of slaves were used to pick cotton.

After the civil war between the northern and southern states was over in 1865, all slaves were freed. But a few years later, state laws were enacted that would take away the rights of African-Americans. These segregation laws restricted the movements of African-Americans in all parts of their lives.

For example, segregation laws determined where African-Americans could sit on buses and trains.

For many years, the front sections of the buses in Montgomery, Alabama were only for white people, as were buses throughout the southern United States.

African-Americans had to pay their fares to the bus driver, then get off the bus and enter again through the rear door. (Sometimes the bus would leave while they were trying to get to the rear door.)

While they were on the bus, African-Americans were expected to give up their seats for any white passenger who wanted to sit down.

On December 1, 1955, Rosa Parks was going home after a long day of work as a seamstress in downtown Montgomery, Alabama. She sat down in the first seat behind the whites-only section.

More passengers got on the bus, and soon every seat was taken. Then the bus driver ordered her to give up her seat for a white man. Mrs. Parks refused, and she was arrested.

That refusal was an important event in American history. African-Americans in Montgomery protested the arrest of Mrs. Parks by refusing to ride the buses. Many people walked miles every day to get to work, as the buses drove by with few passengers. Organized by Reverend Martin Luther King, Jr., the Montgomery bus boycott was in the news all over the world.

Finally, more than a year later, the United States Supreme Court ruled that the bus company couldn't segregate passengers, and African-Americans began riding the bus again.

The Convert
Lerone Bennett, Jr.

A man don't know[1] what he'll do, a man don't know what he is till he gets his back pressed up against a wall.[2] Now you take[3] Aaron Lott: There ain't no other way to explain the crazy thing he did. He was going along fine, preaching[4] the gospel, saving souls, and getting along with[5] the white folks; and then, all of a sudden, he felt wood pressing against his back. The funny thing was that nobody knew he was hurting till he preached that Red Sea sermon[6] where he got mixed up and seemed to think Mississippi was Egypt. As chairman of the deacons board,[7] I felt it was my duty to reason[8] with him. I appreciated his position[9] and told him so, but I didn't think it was right for him to
10 push us all in a hole. The old fool—he just laughed.

"Brother Booker," he said, "The Lord[10]—He'll take care of me."

I knew then that that man was heading for trouble. And the very next thing he did confirmed it. The white folks called the old fool[11] downtown to bear witness[12] that the colored folks[13] were happy. And you know what he did: He got down there amongst all them big white folks and he said: "Things ain't gonna change here overnight, but they gonna change. It's inevitable. The Lord wants it."

Well sir, you could have bought them white folks for a penny. Aaron Lott, pastor of the Rock of Zion Baptist Church, a man white folks had said was wise and sound and sensible, had come close—too close—to saying that the Supreme
20 Court[14] was coming to Melina, Mississippi. The surprising thing was that the white folks didn't do nothing.[15] There was a lot of mumbling and whispering but nothing bad happened till the terrible morning when Aaron came a-knocking at

---

1 man don't know: man doesn't know; this grammatical construction is sometimes used in spoken English in many parts of North America
2 back pressed up against a wall: had no other choice
3 you take: (here) for example
4 preaching: teaching religion as the leader of a church
5 getting along with: having a good relationship with
6 sermon: minister's speech in church
7 deacons board: church administration
8 reason: (here) persuade; convince
9 appreciated his position: understood how he felt
10 the Lord: God

11 old fool: (here) affectionate term for his friend (*fool* is generally used to mean stupid person)
12 bear witness: to say something seriously, promising that it's the truth
13 colored folks: (this term is no longer used) African-Americans
14 Supreme Court: the highest court in the United States. This court had ruled that buses couldn't segregate passengers. However, state and local police and courts were ignoring that ruling.
15 didn't do nothing: didn't do anything; this grammatical construction (double negative) is sometimes used in spoken English in many parts of North America

the door of my funeral home.[16] Now things had been tightening up[17]—you could feel it in the air—and I didn't want no part of no crazy scheme[18] and I told him so right off. He walked on past me and sat down on the couch. He had on his preaching clothes, a shiny blue suit, a fresh starched white shirt, a black tie, and his Sunday black shoes. I remember thinking at the time that Aaron was too black to be wearing all them dark clothes. The thought tickled me and I started to smile but then I noticed something about him that didn't seem quite right. I ran my eyes over him closely. He was kinda middle-sized and he had a big clean-shaven head, a big nose, and thin lips. I stood there looking at him for a long time but I couldn't figure out what it was till I looked at his eyes: They were burning bright, like light bulbs do just before they go out. And yet he looked contented, like his mind was resting somewheres else. **30**

"I wanna talk with you, Booker," he said, glancing sideways at my wife. "If you don't mind, Sister Brown—"

Sarah got up and went into the living quarters. Aaron didn't say nothing for a long time; he just sat there looking out the window. Then he spoke so soft I had to strain my ears to hear.

"I'm leaving for the Baptist convention,"[19] he said. He pulled out his gold watch and looked at it. "Train leaves in 'bout two hours." **40**

"I know *that*, Aaron."

"Yeah, but what I wanted to tell you was that I ain't going Jim Crow.[20] I'm going first class, Booker, right through the white waiting room. That's the law."

A cold shiver[21] ran through me.

"Aaron," I said, "don't you go talking crazy now."

The old fool laughed, a great big body-shaking laugh. He started talking 'bout God and Jesus and all that stuff. Now, I'm a God-fearing man myself, but I holds that God helps those who help themselves. I told him so.

"You can't mix God up with these white folks," I said. "When you start to messing around with segregation,[22] they'll burn you up and the Bible, too." **50**

He looked at me like I was Satan.[23]

"I sweated over this thing," he said. "I prayed.[24] I got down on my knees and I asked God not to give me this cup. But He said I was the one. I heard Him,

---

16 funeral home: a business place where people who have recently died are prepared for burial and ceremonies are held for them before burial
17 things had been tightening up: the atmosphere had been getting tense
18 scheme: plan
19 Baptist convention: meeting of preachers from the Baptist churches
20 Jim Crow: Beginning in the late 1870s, the Jim Crow laws were created throughout the South. These laws specified that African-Americans had to be kept separate from white people. For example, African-Americans had to be in separate cars on a train, and separate waiting rooms had signs indicating "colored" and "white." By 1900, segregation laws were rigidly in place.
21 shiver: shaking feeling from the cold
22 segregation: a system of laws and practices that separate African-Americans in transportation, schools, housing, and jobs
23 Satan: in Christianity, Satan is the representation of evil
24 prayed: communicated with God

Booker, right here—he tapped his chest—in my heart."

The old fool's been having visions,[25] I thought. I sat down and tried to figure out a way to hold him, but he got up, without saying a word, and started for the door.

"Wait!" I shouted. "I'll get my coat."

60   "I don't need you," he said. "I just came by to tell you so you could tell the board in case something happened."

"You wait," I shouted, and ran out of the room to get my coat.

We got in his beat-up old Ford and went by the parsonage[26] to get his suitcase. Rachel—that was his wife—and Jonah were sitting in the living room, wringing their hands. Aaron got his bag, shook Jonah's hand, and said, "Take care of your Mamma, boy." Jonah nodded. Aaron hugged Rachel and pecked at her cheek. Rachel broke down. She threw her arms around his neck and carried on something awful.[27] Aaron shoved her away.

"Don't go making no fuss over it, woman. I ain't gonna be gone forever.
70   Can't a man go to a church meeting 'thout women screaming and crying."

He tried to make light of it, but you could see he was touched by the way his lips trembled. He held his hand out to me, but I wouldn't take it. I told him off good,[28] told him it was a sin and a shame for a man of God to be carrying on like he was, worrying his wife and everything.

"I'm coming with you," I said. "Somebody's gotta see that you don't make a fool of yourself."

He shrugged, picked up his suitcase, and started for the door. Then he stopped and turned around and looked at his wife and his boy and from the way he looked I knew that there was still a chance. He looked at the one and then at the other.
80   For a moment there, I thought he was going to cry, but he turned, quick-like, and walked out of the door.

I ran after him and tried to talk some sense[29] in his head. But he shook me off, turned the corner, and went on up Adams Street. I caught up with him and we walked in silence, crossing the street in front of the First Baptist Church for whites, going on around the Confederate monument where, once, they hung[30] a boy for fooling around with[31] white women.

"Put it off,[32] Aaron," I begged. "Sleep on it."

He didn't say nothing.

"What you need is a vacation. I'll get the board to approve, full pay and
90   everything."

25 having visions: seeing things that aren't there
26 parsonage: minister's home
27 carried on something awful: became very upset
28 told him off good: told him, in a severe and angry manner, that what he was doing was wrong

29 sense: logic; intelligence
30 hung: killed by hanging; beginning in the late nineteenth century, thousands of African-American, mostly men, were killed by mobs of white people in a practice called *lynching*
31 fooling around with: getting involved with
32 put it off: postpone it

He smiled and shifted the suitcase over to his left hand. Big drops of sweat were running down his face and spotting up his shirt. His eyes were awful, all lit up and burning.

"Aaron, Aaron, can't you hear me?"

We passed the feed store, Bill Williams' grocery story, and the movie house.

"A man's gotta think about his family, Aaron. A man ain't free. Didn't you say that once, didn't you?"

He shaded his eyes with his hand and looked into the sun. He put the suitcase on the ground and checked his watch.

"Why don't you think about Jonah?" I asked. "Answer that. Why don't you **100** think about your own son?"

"I am," he said. "That's exactly what I'm doing, thinking about Jonah. Matter of fact, he started *me* to thinking. I ain't never mentioned it before, but the boy's been worrying me. One day we was downtown here and he asked me something that hurt. 'Daddy,' he said, 'how come you ain't a man?' I got mad, I did, and told him: 'I am a man.' He said that wasn't what he meant. 'I mean,' he said, 'how come you ain't a man where white folks concerned.'[33] I couldn't answer him, Booker. I'll never forget it till the day I die. I couldn't answer my own son, and I been preaching forty years."

"He don't know nothing 'bout it," I said. "He's hot-headed, like my boy. He'll **110** find out when he grows up."

"I hopes not," Aaron said, shaking his head. "I hopes not."

Some white folks passed and we shut up till they were out of hearing. Aaron, who was acting real strange, looked up in the sky and moved his lips. He came back to himself, after a little bit, and he said: "This thing of being a man, Booker, is a big thing. The Supreme Court can't make you a man. The NAACP[34] can't do it. God Almighty can do a lot, but even He can't do it. Ain't nobody can do it but you."

He said that like he was preaching and when he got through he was all filled up with emotion and he seemed kind of ashamed—he was a man who didn't like **120** emotion outside the church. He looked at his watch, picked up his bag, and said, "Well, let's git it over with."

We turned into Elm and the first thing I saw at the end of the street was the train station. It was an old red building, flat like a slab. A group of white men were fooling around[35] in front of the door. I couldn't make them out from that distance, but I could tell they weren't the kind of white folks to be fooling around with.

We walked on, passing the dry goods store, the barber shop, and the new

33 white folks [are] concerned: when dealing with whites
34 NAACP: the National Association for the Advancement of Colored People was formed in 1909 to organize African-Americans against discrimination and lynching
35 fooling around: having fun doing nothing in particular

building that was going up. Across the street from that was the sheriff's office. I
130 looked in the window and saw Bull Sampson sitting at his desk, his feet propped
up on a chair, a fat brown cigar sticking out of his mouth. A ball about the size of
a sweet potato started burning in my stomach.

"Please Aaron," I said. "Please. You can't get away with it. I know how you
feel. Sometimes I feel the same way myself, but I wouldn't risk my neck to do
nothing for these niggers.[36] They won't appreciate it; they'll laugh at you."

We were almost to the station and I could make out the faces of the men
sitting on the benches. One of them must have been telling a joke. He finished
and the group broke out laughing.

I whispered to Aaron: "I'm through with it. I wash my hands of[37] the whole
140 mess."

I don't know whether he heard me or not. He turned to the right without
saying a word and went on in the front door. The string-beany man who told the
joke was so shocked that his cigarette fell out of his mouth.

"Y'all see that," he said. "Why, I'll—"

"Shut up," another man said. "Go git Bull."

I kept walking, fast, turned at the corner, and ran around to the colored
waiting room. When I got in there, I looked through the ticket window and saw
Aaron standing in front of the clerk. Aaron stood there for a minute or more, but
the clerk didn't see him. And that took some not seeing.[38] In that room, Aaron
150 Lott stood out like a pig in a chicken coop.

There were, I'd say, about ten or fifteen people in there, but didn't none of
them move. They just sat there, with their eyes glued on Aaron's back. Aaron
cleared his throat. The clerk didn't look up; he got real busy with some papers.
Aaron cleared his throat again and opened his mouth to speak. The screen door of
the waiting room opened and clattered shut.

It got real quiet in that room, hospital quiet. It got so quiet I could hear my
own heart beating. Now Aaron knew who opened that door, but he didn't bat an
eyelid.[39] He turned around real slow and faced High Sheriff[40] Sampson, the
baddest man in south Mississippi.

160 Mr. Sampson stood there with his legs wide open, like the men you see on
television. His beefy face was blood-red and his gray eyes were rattlesnake hard.
He was mad; no doubt about it. I had never seen him so mad.

"Preacher," he said, "you done gone crazy?" He was talking low-like and
mean.

"Nosir," Aaron said. "Nosir, Mr. Sampson."

"What you think you doing?"

---

36 niggers: insulting term for African-
Americans
37 wash my hands of: won't be involved with
anymore

38 that took some not seeing: that was hard
to avoid seeing
39 didn't bat an eyelid: didn't move at all
40 sheriff: the chief police officer in this town

"Going to St. Louis, Mr. Sampson."

"You must done lost yo' mind, boy."[41]

Mr. Sampson started walking towards Aaron with his hand on his gun. Twenty or thirty men pushed through the front door and fanned out over the room. Mr. Sampson stopped about two paces from Aaron and looked him up and down. That look had paralyzed[42] hundreds of niggers; but it didn't faze Aaron none—he stood his ground.

"I'm gonna give you a chance, preacher. Git on over to the nigger side and git quick."

"I ain't bothering nobody, Mr. Sampson."

Somebody in the crowd yelled: "Don't reason wit' the nigger, Bull. Hit 'cm."

Mr. Sampson walked up to Aaron and grabbed him in the collar and throwed him up against the ticket counter. He pulled out his gun.

"Did you hear me, deacon. I said, 'Git.'"

"I'm going to St. Louis, Mr. Sampson. That's cross state lines.[43] The court done said — "

Aaron didn't have a chance. The blow came from nowhere. Laying there on the floor with blood spurting from his mouth, Aaron looked up at Mr. Sampson and he did another crazy thing: he grinned. Bull Sampson jumped up in the air and came down on Aaron with all his two hundred pounds. It made a crunchy sound. He jumped again and the mob, maddened by the blood and heat, moved in to help him. They fell on Aaron like mad dogs. They beat him with chairs; they beat him with sticks; they beat him with guns.

Till this day, I don't know what come over me.[44] The first thing I know I was running and then I was standing in the middle of the white waiting room. Mr. Sampson was the first to see me. He backed off, cocked his pistol,[45] and said: "Booker, boy, you come one mo' step and I'll kill you. What's a matter with you niggers today? All y'all gone crazy?"

"Please don't kill him," I begged. "You ain't got no call to treat him like that."

"So you saw it all, did you? Well, then, Booker you musta saw the nigger preacher reach for my gun?"

"He didn't do that, Mr. Sampson," I said. "He didn't—"

Mr. Sampson put a big hairy hand on my tie and pulled me to him.

"Booker," he said sweetly. "You saw the nigger preacher reach for my gun, didn't you?"

I didn't open my mouth—I couldn't I was so scared—but I guess my eyes answered for me. Whatever Mr. Sampson saw there musta convinced him 'cause he throwed me on the floor besides Aaron.

---

41 boy: an insulting way whites addressed adult African-American men
42 paralyzed: unable to move
43 cross state lines: segregation on buses between states (interstate transportation) was ruled illegal by the U.S. Supreme Court
44 what came over me: what made me do what I did
45 pistol: gun

"Git this nigger out of here," he said, "and be quick about it."

Dropping to my knees, I put my hand on Aaron's chest; I didn't feel nothing. I felt his wrist; I didn't feel nothing. I got up and looked at them white folks with tears in my eyes. I looked at the women, sitting crying on the benches. I looked at the men. I looked at Mr. Sampson. I said, "He was a good man."

210   Mr. Sampson said, "Move the nigger."

A big sigh came out of me and I wrung my hands.

Mr. Sampson said, "Move the nigger."

He grabbed my tie and twisted it, but I didn't feel nothing. My eyes were glued to his hands; there was blood under the fingernails, and the fingers—they looked like fat little red sausages. I screamed and Mr. Sampson flung me down on the floor.

He said, *"Move the nigger."*

I picked Aaron up and fixed his body over my shoulder and carried him outside. I sent for one of my boys and we dressed him up[46] and put him away real
220 nice-like and Rachel and the boy came and they cried and carried on and yet, somehow, they seemed prouder of Aaron than ever before. And the colored folks—they seemed proud, too. Crazy niggers. Didn't they know? Couldn't they see? It hadn't done no good. In fact, things got worse. The Northern newspapers[47] started kicking up a stink and Mr. Rivers, the solicitor,[48] announced they were going to hold a hearing.[49] All of a sudden, Booker Taliaferro Brown[50] became the biggest man in that town. My phone rang day and night: I got threats,[51] I got promises, and I was offered bribes.[52] Everywhere I turned somebody was waiting to ask me: "Whatcha gonna do? Whatcha gonna say?" To tell the truth, I didn't know myself.[53] One day I would decide one thing and the next day I would decide
230 another.

It was Mr. Rivers and Mr. Sampson who called my attention to that. They came to my office one day and called me a shifty, no-good nigger. They said they expected me to stand by "my statement"[54] in the train station that I saw Aaron reach for the gun. I hadn't said no such thing, but Mr. Sampson said I said it and he said he had witnesses[55] who heard me say it. "And if you say anything else," he said, "I can't be responsible for your health. Now you know"—he put that

46 dressed him up: (here) put him in nice clothes for his funeral and burial
47 Northern newspapers: newspapers from cities in the north of the United States such as New York or Chicago; in writing about segregation in the South, these newspapers would generally be more sympathetic to African-Americans
48 solicitor: the chief law officer in this town
49 hold a hearing: hold a meeting to investigate
50 Booker Taliaferro Brown: the story's narrator, named after Booker T. Washington, a leader of African-Americans in the late nineteenth century. Booker T. Washington developed the Tuskegee Institute in Alabama for African-Americans, and his philosophy emphasized education for African-Americans rather than political struggle for civil rights.
51 threat: promise to cause pain
52 bribe: money paid to get someone to do something illegal or wrong
53 I didn't know myself: (here) even I wasn't sure
54 stand by my statement: not change my statement
55 witnesses: people who saw the incident happen

bloody hand on my shoulder and he smiled his sweet death smile—"you *know* I wouldn't threaten you, but the boys"—he shook his head—"the boys are real worked up[56] over this one."

It was long about then that I began to hate Aaron Lott. I'm ashamed to admit **240** it now, but it's true: I hated him. He had lived his life; he had made his choice. Why should he live my life, too, and make me choose? It wasn't fair; it wasn't right; it wasn't Christian. What made me so mad was the fact that nothing I said would help Aaron. He was dead and it wouldn't help one whit for me to say he didn't reach for that gun. I tried to explain that to Rachel when she came to my office, moaning and crying, the night before the hearing.

"Listen to me, woman," I said. "Listen. Aaron was a good man. He lived a good life. He did a lot of good things, but he's *dead, dead, dead!* Nothing I say will bring him back. Bull Sampson's got ten niggers who are going to swear on a stack of Bibles that they saw Aaron reach for that gun. It won't do me or you or **250** Aaron no good for me to swear otherwise."

What did I say that for? That woman liked to had a fit.[57] She got down on her knees and she begged me to go with Aaron.

"Go wit' him," she cried. "Booker, *Booker!* If you's a man, if you's a father, if you's a friend, go wit' Aaron."

That woman tore my heart up. I ain't never heard nobody beg like that.

"Tell the truth, Booker," she said. "That's all I'm asking. Tell the truth."

"Truth!" I said, "Hah! That's all you niggers talk about: truth. What do you know about truth? Truth is eating good and sleeping good. Truth is living, Rachel. Be loyal to the living." **260**

Rachel backed off from me. You would have thought that I had cursed her or something. She didn't say nothing; she just stood there pressed against the door. She stood there saying nothing for so long that my nerves snapped.

"Say something," I shouted. "Say something—anything!"

She shook her head, slowly at first, and then her head started moving like it wasn't attached to her body. It went back and forth, back and forth, back and forth. I started towards her, but she jerked open the door and ran out into the night, screaming.

That did it. I ran across the room to the filing cabinet, opened the bottom drawer, and took out a dusty bottle of Scotch.[58] I started drinking, but the more I **270** drank the soberer I got. I guess I fell asleep 'cause I dreamed I buried Rachel and that everything went along fine until she jumped out of the casket and started screaming. I came awake with a start and knocked over the bottle. I reached for a rag and my hand stopped in midair.

"Of course," I said out loud and slammed my fist down on the Scotch-soaked papers.

56 worked up: upset **58 Scotch:** a kind of whiskey
57 had a fit: (here) became very upset

I didn't see nothing.
Why didn't I think of it before?
I didn't see nothing.
Jumping up, I walked to and fro in the office. Would it work? I rehearsed it in
280 my mind. All I could see was Aaron's back. I don't know whether he reached for
the gun or not. All I know is that *for some reason* the men beat him to death.

Rehearsing the thing in my mind, I felt a great weight slip off my shoulders. I
did a little jig[59] in the middle of the floor and went upstairs to my bed, whistling.
Sarah turned over and looked me up and down.

"What you happy about?"

"Can't a man be happy?" I asked.

She sniffed the air, said, "Oh," turned over, and mumbled something in her
pillow. It came to me then for the first time that she was 'bout the only person in
town who hadn't asked me what I was going to do. I thought about it for a little
290 while, shrugged, and fell into bed with all my clothes on.

When I woke up the next morning, I had a terrible headache and my tongue
was a piece of sandpaper. For a long while, I couldn't figure out what I was doing
laying there with all my clothes on. Then it came to me: This was the big day. I
put on my black silk suit, the one I wore for big funerals, and went downstairs to
breakfast. I walked into the dining room without looking and bumped into
Russell, the last person in the world I wanted to see. He was my only child, but he
didn't act like it. He was always finding fault.[60] He didn't like the way I talked to
Negroes; he didn't like the way I talked to white folks. He didn't like this; he
didn't like that. And to top it off, the young whippersnapper wanted to be an
300 artist. Undertaking[61] wasn't good enough for him. He wanted to paint pictures.

I sat down and grunted.

"Good morning, Papa." He said it like he meant it. He wants something, I
thought, looking him over closely, noticing that his right eye was swollen.

"You been fighting again, boy?"

"Yes, Papa."

"You younguns. Education—that's what it is. Education! It's ruining you."

He didn't say nothing. He just sat there, looking down when I looked up and
looking up when I looked down. This went on through the grits and the eggs and
the second cup of coffee.

310 "Whatcha looking at?" I asked.

"Nothing, Papa."

"Whatcha thinking?"

"Nothing, Papa."

"You lying, boy. It's written all over your face."

---

59 jig: a dance
60 finding fault: finding something wrong

61 undertaking: the profession of arranging
funerals and burials

He didn't say nothing.

I dismissed him with a wave of my hand, picked up the paper, and turned to the sports page.

"What are you going to do, Papa?"

The question caught me unawares. I know now that I was expecting it, that I wanted him to ask it; but he put it so bluntly that I was flabbergasted.[62] I **320** pretended I didn't understand.

"Do 'bout what, boy? Speak up!"

"About the trial, Papa."

I didn't say nothing for a long time. There wasn't much, in fact, I could say; so I got mad.

"Questions, questions, questions," I shouted. "That's all I get in this house—questions. You never have a civil word[63] for your pa. I go out of here and work my tail off and you keep yourself shut up in that room of yours looking at them fool books and now soon as your old man gets his back against the wall you join the pack. I expected better than that of you, boy. A son ought to back his pa."[64]   **330**

That hurt him. He picked up the coffee pot and poured himself another cup of coffee and his hand trembled. He took a sip and watched me over the rim.

"They say you are going to chicken out,[65] Papa."

"Chicken out? What that mean?"

"They're betting you'll 'Tom.'"[66]

I leaned back in the chair and took a sip of coffee.

"So they're betting, huh?" The idea appealed to me. "Crazy niggers—they'd bet on a funeral."

I saw pain on his face. He sighed and said: "I bet, too, Papa."

The cup fell out of my hand and broke, spilling black water over the **340** tablecloth.

"You did what?"

"I bet you wouldn't 'Tom.'"

"You little fool." I fell out laughing and then I stopped suddenly and looked at him closely. "How much you bet?"

"One hundred dollars."

I stood up.

"You're lying," I said. "Where'd you get that kind of money?"

"From Mamma."

"Sarah!" I shouted. "Sarah! You get in here. What kind of house you running, **350**

---

62 flabbergasted: very surprised
63 civil word: speech that isn't angry
64 back his pa: support his father
65 chicken out: (slang) become afraid
66 Tom: comes from "Uncle Tom," a negative term used in the African-American community to describe a man who only does what white people want. *Uncle Tom's Cabin* by Harriet Beecher Stowe was a popular book at the time of the American Civil War. Although the book spoke out against slavery, it also described African-American adults as though they were children.

sneaking behind my back, giving this boy money to gamble with?"

Sarah leaned against the door jamb. She was in her hot iron mood. There was no expression on her face. And her eyes were hard.

"I gave it to him, Booker," she said. "They called you an Uncle Tom. He got in a fight about it. He wanted to bet on you, Booker. *He* believes in you."

Suddenly I felt old and used up. I pulled a chair to me and sat down.

"Please," I said, waving my hand. "Please. Go away. Leave me alone. Please."

I sat there for maybe ten or fifteen minutes, thinking, praying. The phone 360 rang. It was Mr. Withers, the president of the bank. I had put in for a loan and it had been turned down,[67] but Mr. Withers said there'd been a mistake. "New fellow, you know," he said, clucking his tongue. He said he knew that it was my lifelong dream to build a modern funeral home and to buy a Cadillac hearse. He said he sympathized with that dream, supported it, thought the town needed it, and thought I deserved it. "The loan will go through," he said. "Drop by and see me this morning after the hearing."

When I put that phone down, it was wet with sweat. I couldn't turn that new funeral home down and Mr. Withers knew it. My father had raised me on that dream and before he died he made me swear on a Bible that I would make it 370 good. And here it was on a platter,[68] just for a word, a word that wouldn't hurt nobody.

I put on my hat and hurried to the courthouse. When they called my name, I walked in with my head held high.[69] The courtroom was packed.[70] The white folks had all the seats and the colored folks were standing in the rear. Whoever arranged the seating had set aside the first two rows for white men. They were sitting almost on top of each other, looking mean and uncomfortable in their best white shirts.

I walked up to the bench and swore on the Bible and took a seat. Mr. Rivers gave me a little smile and waited for me to get myself set.

380   "State your name," he said.

"Booker Taliaferro Brown." I took a quick look at the first two rows and recognized at least ten of the men who killed Aaron.

"And your age?"

"Fifty-seven."

"You're an undertaker?"

"Yessir."

"You been living in this town all your life?"

"Yessir."

---

67 turned down: denied; refused
68 on a platter: given easily; a platter is a large plate
69 head held high: proudly
70 packed: (here) very crowded

"You like it here, don't you, Booker?"

Was this a threat? I looked Mr. Rivers in the face for the first time. He smiled. 390
I told the truth. I said, "Yessir."

"Now, calling your attention to the day of May 17th, did anything unusual happen on that day?"

The question threw me.[71] I shook my head. Then it dawned on me. He was talking about—

"Yessir," I said. "That's the day Aaron got —" Something in Mr. Rivers' face warned me and I pulled up —"that's the day of the trouble at the train station."

Mr. Rivers smiled. He looked like a trainer who'd just put a monkey through a new trick. You could feel the confidence and the contempt oozing out of him. I looked at his prissy little mustache and his smiling lips and I got mad. Lifting my 400
head a little bit, I looked him full in the eyes; I held the eyes for a moment and I tried to tell the man behind the eyes that I was a man like him and that he didn't have no right to be using me and laughing about it. But he didn't get the message. The bastard[72]— he chuckled[73] softly, turned his back to me, and faced the audience.

"I believe you were with the preacher that day."

The water was getting deep. I scrooched down in my seat, closed the lids of my eyes, and looked dense.[74]

"Yessir, Mr. Rivers," I drawled. "Ah was, Ah was."

"Now, Booker—" he turned around— "I believe you tried to keep the nigger 410
preacher from getting out of line."[75]

I hesitated. It wasn't a fair question. Finally, I said: "Yessir."

"You begged him not to go in the white side?"

"Yessir."

"And when that failed, you went over to *your* side—the *colored* side—and looked through the window?"

"Yessir."

He put his hand in his coat pocket and studied my face.

"You saw *everything*, didn't you?"

"Just about." A muscle on the inside of my thigh started tingling. 420

Mr. Rivers shuffled some papers he had in his hand. He seemed to be thinking real hard. I pushed myself against the back of the chair. Mr. Rivers moved close, quick, and stabbed his finger into my chest.

"Booker, did you see the nigger preacher reach for Mr. Sampson's gun?"

He backed away, smiling. I looked away from him and felt my heart trying to tear out of my skin. I looked out over the courtroom. It was still; wasn't even a fly

---

71 threw me: (here) confused me
72 bastard: (here) an insulting term for someone
73 chuckled: laughed quietly

74 dense: (here) stupid
75 getting out of line: (here) doing the wrong thing

moving. I looked at the white folks in front and the colored folks in back and I turned the question over in my mind. While I was doing that, waiting, taking my time, I noticed, out of the corner of my eye, that the smile on Mr. Rivers' face

430   was dying away. Suddenly, I had a terrible itch[76] to know what that smile would turn into.

I said, "Nosir."

Mr. Rivers stumbled backwards like he had been shot. Old Judge Sloan took off his glasses and pushed his head out over the bench. The whole courtroom seemed to be leaning in to me and I saw Aaron's widow leaning back with her eyes closed and it seemed to me at that distance that her lips were moving in prayer.

Mr. Rivers was the first to recover. He put his smile back on and he acted like my answer was in the script.[77]

440   "You mean," he said, "that you didn't see it. It happened so quickly that you missed it?"

I looked at the bait[78] and I ain't gonna lie: I was tempted. He knew as well as I did what I meant, but he was gambling on my weakness. I had thrown away my funeral home, my hearse, everything I owned, and he was standing there like a magician, pulling them out of a hat, one at a time, dangling them, saying: "Looka here, looka here, don't they look pretty?" I was on top of a house and he was betting that if he gave me a ladder I would come down. He was wrong, but you can't fault him for trying. He hadn't never met no nigger who would go all the way. I looked him in the eye and went the last mile.

450   "Aaron didn't reach for that gun," I said. "Them people, they just fell on—"

"Hold it," he shouted. "I want to remind you that there are laws in this state against perjury.[79] You can go to jail for five years for what you just said. Now I know you've been conferring with those NAACP fellows, but I want to remind you of the statements you made to Sheriff Sampson and me. Judge—" he dismissed me with a wave of his hand— "Judge, this *man*—" he caught himself and it was my turn to smile—"this *boy* is lying. Ten niggers have testified that they saw the preacher reach for the gun. Twenty white people saw it. You've heard their testimony. I want to withdraw this witness and I want to reserve the right to file perjury charges against him."

460   Judge Sloan nodded. He pushed his bottom lip over his top one.

"You can step down," he said. "I want to warn you that perjury is a very grave offense. You—"

"Judge, I didn't—"

"Nigger!" He banged his gavel. "Don't you interrupt me. Now git out of here."

---

76 itch: desire to scratch, such as when you have an insect bite
77 script: written lines of a drama, theater
78 bait: (here) opportunity, temptation
79 perjury: telling a lie under oath in court

Two guards pushed me outside and waved away the reporters. Billy Giles, Mr. Sampson's assistant, came out and told me Mr. Sampson wanted me out of town before sundown. "And he says you'd better get out before the Northern reporters leave. He won't be responsible for your safety after that."

I nodded and went on down the stairs and started out the door. **470**

"Booker!"

Rachel and a whole line of Negroes were running down the stairs. I stepped outside and waited for them. Rachel ran up and throwed her arms around me. "It don't take but one, Booker," she said. "It don't take but one."[80] Somebody else said: "They whitewashed[81] it, they whitewashed it, but you spoiled it for 'em."

Russell came out then and stood over to the side while the others crowded around to shake my hands. Then the others sensed that he was waiting and they made a little aisle. He walked up to me kind of slow-like and he said, "Thank you, sir." That was the first time in his whole seventeen years that that boy had said "sir" to me. I cleared my throat and when I opened my eyes Sarah was **480**
standing beside me. She didn't say nothing; she just put her hand in mine and stood there. It was long about then, I guess, when I realized that I wasn't seeing so good. They say I cried, but I don't believe a word of it. It was such a hot day and the sun was shining so bright that the sweat rolling down my face blinded me. I wiped the sweat out of my eyes and some more people came up and said a lot of foolish things about me showing the white folks and following in Aaron's footsteps.[82] I wasn't doing no such fool thing. Ol' Man Rivers just put the thing to me in a way it hadn't been put before—man to man. It was simple, really. Any man would have done it.

---

80 it don't take but one: only one person is needed
81 whitewashed: covered up the truth

82 following in Aaron's footsteps: following Aaron's example

Understanding the Story

Work individually or with another student to answer these comprehension questions and review the story's events.

1. What kind of work did Aaron Lott do? What is the occupation of Booker T. Brown, the narrator of the story?

2. What was unusual about Aaron's plan to travel to the Baptist convention? How did Booker and Sarah (Aaron's wife) feel about Aaron's travel plan?

3. What was the question Aaron's son asked that Aaron couldn't answer?

4. How did the white men react when they saw Aaron enter the white waiting room?

5. What did Bull Sampson do to the preacher?

6. What was Bull Sampson's version of the event?

7. How did Booker feel about what Aaron had done?

8. What decision did Booker struggle to make? Why was it so hard to make this decision?

9. What was the bet that Booker's son made?

10. Why did Mr. Withers of the bank call Booker? Why did this make it more difficult for Booker to decide?

11. What was the opportunity that Mr. Rivers offered Booker on the witness stand?

Talking and Writing

With your classmates, use these questions as starting points for a discussion of ideas presented in the story. Then select a question and write an essay on the topic.

1. What were the results of Booker's decision to tell what he saw at the train station? What were the reactions of the judge, the sheriff, the community? Do you think Booker stayed in Melina or went north? Why?

   What do you think of the reaction of Booker's son to Booker's decision?

2. What does the first sentence of the story mean? What would you have done in Booker's place?

   Do you think Booker's actions would have been justified if the result was that a member of his family was jailed or killed? (Would you have done the same thing?)

3. Why did the author choose this title for the story? With so many forces influencing Booker, what do you think was the most important reason Booker changed his mind? Why? (What does the last line of the story mean?)

4. How does the author show the atmosphere of fear when Aaron walks into the train station? How does the author create suspense when Booker is testifying in the courtroom? What keeps you wondering what Booker will do? How do you know that Booker is afraid?

5. In what ways do other societies have conditions that are similar to the situation described in this story? Why would people want to keep a system that excludes some of the population?

What do you think the whites in Melina were afraid of? For example, how would legal equality of black Americans affect them economically?

6. Can human behavior be changed by laws? Why or why not? Was nonviolence an appropriate strategy for the situation in this story? When is nonviolence an effective method of achieving justice? What happens if nonviolence doesn't work?

7. What other groups in the world have struggled to gain their rights? What tactics have they used? Do you agree with their methods? Are they effective?

More Ideas

1. Write a short paper explaining a moral choice you or someone else had to make.

2. Write a short paper about someone you know, or about someone famous in history, who has done something heroic, such as publicly support an unpopular position, or give up a job because the work was immoral, or choose to help people despite physical danger.

3. Libraries and bookstores will have books about the civil rights movement and African-American history in the United States.

Suggested non-fiction and historical reading: *Children of Crisis* by Robert Coles; *The Autobiography of Malcolm X* with Alex Haley; *The Long Shadow of Little Rock* by Daisy Bates.

Eyes on the Prize (by Juan Williams, with the production staff at Blackside, Inc.) is a book and also a video that describes the civil rights movement, using news films from the era and interviews with people who participated in that movement. The movie *The Long Walk Home* (starring Whoopi Goldberg) describes the Montgomery bus boycott.

Suggested fictional and autobiographical reading: *Going to Meet the Man* by James Baldwin; *Manchild in a Promised Child* by Claude Brown; *I Know Why the Caged Bird Sings* by Maya Angelou. *Black-Eyed Susans/Midnight Birds* is a collection of short stories by black women, edited by Mary Helen Washington.

4. You may have already heard of the following people. Find out why one of them was important in American history and tell the class, or write a short paper.

   Martin Luther King   Thurgood Marshall

   James Meredith   Malcolm X

   Ku Klux Klan   Freedom Riders

5. Check newspapers and magazines for descriptions of new laws or events that show how the civil rights movement has affected the United States.

Building Vocabulary

Summarize what happened in this story, using some of the following words. Be sure to change the form of the word, if necessary.

preacher	Supreme Court	funeral home
scheme	bribe	turn down
packed	bait	perjury
tell him off	wash my hands of	threats
hold high	witnesses	follow in his footsteps

1. Aaron was a _____ who planned to take the train to the Baptist convention. He planned to go through the white waiting room.

2. Booker said he didn't want to be part of Aaron's crazy _____. Booker knew that a black man could be killed for using the white waiting room, even though segregation on trains had been declared illegal by the United States _____.

3. Booker tried to reason with Aaron, but Aaron was determined to challenge segregation. Booker was angry with Aaron, so he _____.

4. Booker's job was at a _____. He had applied for a loan at the bank, but it had been _____. Booker got a call from the bank: If Booker didn't tell the truth in court, he'd get the loan.

5. Booker got calls promising money, or _____, if he'd lie in court.

6. When Booker went to the courtroom, he felt proud. He had his head _____.

7. There were a lot of people in the courtroom. The room was _____.

8. When Booker told the truth, the judge accused him of _____.

9. After Booker told the truth, people in the community spoke of Aaron. They said Booker was _____.

The Man to Send Rain Clouds

Leslie Silko

Before You Begin . . .

The following story shows ways in which some modern American Indians keep their native traditions, while adopting some of the customs of the white man.

Born in 1948, Leslie Silko grew up on the Laguna Pueblo reservation in New Mexico, in the American Southwest.

Silko writes short stories and poetry and is the first native American woman to have published a novel (*Ceremony*). Her writing includes traditional Indian folklore and legends, as well as descriptions of modern Indian life.

The Pueblo Indians in New Mexico and Arizona are best known for the cliff villages of their ancestors. They're also known for their community houses of stone or adobe that are often several stories high.

The word *pueblo* means *town* in Spanish. Because Spain and, later, Mexico explored and occupied the region, and because Mexico is near the southwest United States, many names and common words in this area were originally Spanish.

Before reading this story, your class could briefly discuss what happens to a community when it's conquered by another group of people. What can be done to keep a culture from disappearing?

You'll find it helpful to read this story twice: once to get an overview of what's happening, and again to understand more of the story's meaning and appreciate the author's style.

When Christopher Columbus traveled west from Europe and arrived in America in 1492, he incorrectly thought he had reached India. He met the people who were the natives of North America and called them *Indians*.

The first people on the North American continent and their descendants are usually referred to as American Indians and Canadian Indians, or as native Americans and native Canadians.

You'll also hear about specific groups of Indians. For example, the Cree, Dene, and Ojibway Indians live in what is now Canada, and the Mohawk, Cheyenne, and Cherokee Indians live in what is now the United States.

For many centuries before the arrival of Europeans, the Indians had developed their own cultures and languages all over North America.

Some Indians were hunters, some were farmers, some were warriors, some were peaceful. In general, they shared a point of view about the land that was very different from the attitude of the Europeans who came later. The Indians felt that they were living in harmony with nature, while the Europeans who settled in North America wanted to win the war against nature.

After Europeans began arriving in the late fifteenth century, they fought with the Indians to gain ownership of land. War and starvation killed large segments of the Indian population. The European settlers were determined to force the Indians to give up their way of life.

Indians were forced to leave their lands to live on reservations, or reserves, which were areas of land the white man in North America didn't want.

The Man to Send Rain Clouds

Leslie Silko

ONE

They found him under a big cottonwood tree.[1] His Levi jacket[2] and pants were faded light-blue so that he had been easy to find. The big cottonwood tree stood apart from a small grove of winterbare[3] cottonwoods which grew in the wide, sandy arroyo.[4] He had been dead for a day or more, and the sheep had wandered[5] and scattered[6] up and down the arroyo. Leon and his brother-in-law, Ken, gathered the sheep and left them in the pen[7] at the sheep camp before they returned to the cottonwood tree. Leon waited under the tree while Ken drove the truck through the deep sand to the edge of the arroyo. He squinted up at the sun and unzipped his jacket—it sure was hot for this time of year. But high and northwest the blue mountains were still deep in snow. Ken came sliding down the low, crumbling bank[8] about fifty yards down, and he was bringing the red blanket.

Before they wrapped the old man, Leon took a piece of string out of his pocket and tied a small gray feather in the old man's long white hair. Ken gave him the paint. Across the brown wrinkled forehead he drew a streak of white and along the high cheekbones he drew a strip of blue paint. He paused and watched Ken throw pinches of corn meal[9] and pollen into the wind that fluttered the small gray feather. Then Leon painted with yellow under the old man's broad nose, and finally, when he had painted green across the chin, he smiled.

"Send us rain clouds, Grandfather." They laid the bundle[10] in the back of the pickup[11] and covered it with a heavy tarp[12] before they started back to the pueblo.

They turned off the highway onto the sandy pueblo road. Not long after they passed the store and post office they saw Father Paul's car coming toward them. When he recognized their faces he slowed his car and waved for them to stop. The young priest rolled down the car window.

"Did you find old Teofilo?" he asked loudly.

---

1 cottonwood tree: kind of tree that has seeds like cotton
2 Levi jacket: short coat made of the same material as blue jeans
3 winterbare: without leaves because of the cold season
4 wide, sandy arroyo: (here) *arroyo* is used to mean "a place where a very small river had dried up." In Spanish, *arroyo* means "a creek or very small river."
5 wandered: traveled with no specific direction
6 scattered: separated in different directions
7 pen: (here) area with a fence around it for keeping animals
8 bank: (here) side of a river
9 pinches of corn meal: very small amounts of ground-up corn, used as flour
10 bundle: package
11 pickup: small truck
12 tarp: material that resists water

56

Leon stopped the truck. "Good morning, Father. We were just out to the sheep camp. Everything is O.K. now."

"Thank God for that. Teofilo is a very old man. You really shouldn't allow him to stay at the sheep camp alone."

30

"No, he won't do that anymore now."

"Well, I'm glad you understand. I hope I'll be seeing you at Mass[13] this week—we missed you last Sunday. See if you can get old Teofilo to come with you." The priest smiled and waved at them as they drove away.

TWO

Louise and Teresa were waiting. The table was set for lunch, and the coffee was boiling on the black iron stove. Leon looked at Louise and then at Teresa.

"We found him under a cottonwood tree in the big arroyo near sheep camp. I guess he sat down to rest in the shade and never got up again." Leon walked toward the old man's bed. The red plaid shawl[14] had been shaken and spread carefully over the bed, and a new brown flannel shirt and pair of stiff new Levis **40** were arranged neatly beside the pillow. Louise held the screen door open while Leon and Ken carried in the red blanket. He looked small and shriveled,[15] and after they dressed him in the new shirt and pants he seemed more shrunken.[16]

It was noontime now because the church bells rang the Angelus.[17] They ate the beans with hot bread, and nobody said anything until after Teresa poured the coffee.

Ken stood up and put on his jacket. "I'll see about the gravediggers.[18] Only the top layer of soil is frozen. I think it can be ready before dark."

Leon nodded his head and finished his coffee. After Ken had been gone for a while, the neighbors and clanspeople[19] came quietly to embrace Teofilo's family **50** and to leave food on the table because the gravediggers would come to eat when they were finished.

THREE

The sky in the west was full of pale-yellow light. Louise stood outside with her hands in the pockets of Leon's green army jacket that was too big for her. The funeral[20] was over, and the old men had taken their candles and medicine bags and were gone. She waited until the body was laid into the pickup before she said

13 Mass: religious service of the community's Catholic Church, administered by the priest
14 shawl: a piece of cloth worn on the head and shoulders
15 shriveled: wrinkled and small
16 shrunken: smaller than before
17 Angelus: an old Catholic tradition of prayer twice a day
18 gravediggers: people who prepare a grave

in which to bury the dead
19 clanspeople: members of a large extended family
20 funeral: religious service in honor of someone who has just died; in this Indian funeral, the old men of the community use candles and sacred objects that they carry in their medicine bags as part of the Indian burial ritual

anything to Leon. She touched his arm, and he noticed that her hands were still dusty from the corn meal that she had sprinkled around the old man. When she spoke, Leon could not hear her.

60   "What did you say? I didn't hear you."

"I said that I had been thinking about something."

"About what?"

"About the priest sprinkling holy water[21] for Grandpa. So he won't be thirsty."

Leon stared at the new moccasins[22] that Teofilo had made for the ceremonial dances[23] in the summer. They were nearly hidden by the red blanket. It was getting colder, and the wind pushed gray dust down the narrow pueblo road. The sun was approaching the long mesa[24] where it disappeared during the winter. Louise stood there shivering and watching his face. Then he zipped up his jacket and opened the truck door. "I'll see if he's there."

FOUR

70   Ken stopped the pickup at the church, and Leon got out; and then Ken drove down the hill to the graveyard where people were waiting. Leon knocked at the old carved door with its symbols of the Lamb.[25] While he waited he looked up at the twin bells from the king of Spain with the last sunlight pouring around them in their tower.

The priest opened the door and smiled when he saw who it was. "Come in! What brings you here this evening?"

The priest walked toward the kitchen, and Leon stood with his cap[26] in his hand, playing with the earflaps and examining the living room—the brown sofa, the green armchair, and the brass lamp that hung down from the ceiling by links

80 of chain. The priest dragged a chair out of the kitchen and offered it to Leon.

"No thank you, Father. I only came to ask you if you would bring your holy water to the graveyard."

The priest turned away from Leon and looked out the window at the patio full of shadows and the dining-room windows of the nuns' cloister across the patio. The curtains were heavy, and the light from within faintly penetrated; it was impossible to see the nuns inside eating supper. "Why didn't you tell me he was dead? I could have brought the Last Rites[27] anyway."

Leon smiled. "It wasn't necessary, Father."

21 sprinkling holy water: a Roman Catholic practice of providing spiritual blessing
22 moccasins: Indian shoes, made of soft leather
23 ceremonial dances: traditional dances held with special clothing and masks to celebrate events, seasons, or a spiritual belief
24 mesa: kind of hill that has a flat top and sharp sides, commonly found in the southwestern United States. The word *mesa* means *table* in Spanish.
25 symbols of the Lamb: (here) the lamb (baby sheep) symbolizes Jesus, the son of God in the Christian religion
26 cap: small, casual type of hat
27 Last Rites: ritual performed by a Catholic priest for sick or dying people

The priest stared down at his scuffed[28] brown loafers[29] and the worn hem of his cassock.[30] "For a Christian burial[31] it was necessary."

His voice was distant, and Leon thought that his blue eyes looked tired.

"It's O.K. Father, we just want him to have plenty of water."

The priest sank down into the green chair and picked up a glossy missionary[32] magazine. He turned the colored pages full of lepers[33] and pagans[34] without looking at them.

"You know I can't do that, Leon. There should have been the Last Rites and a funeral Mass at the very least."

Leon put on his green cap and pulled the flaps down over his ears. "It's getting late, Father. I've got to go."

When Leon opened the door Father Paul stood up and said, "Wait." He left the room and came back wearing a long brown overcoat. He followed Leon out the door and across the dim churchyard to the adobe steps in front of the church. They both stooped to fit through the low adobe entrance. And when they started down the hill to the graveyard only half of the sun was visible above the mesa.

The priest approached the grave slowly, wondering how they had managed to dig into the frozen ground; and then he remembered that this was New Mexico, and saw the pile of cold loose sand beside the hole. The people stood close to each other with little clouds of steam puffing from their faces. The priest looked at them and saw a pile of jackets, gloves, and scarves in the yellow, dry tumbleweeds that grew in the graveyard. He looked at the red blanket, not sure that Teofilo was so small, wondering if it wasn't some perverse[35] Indian trick—something they did in March to ensure a good harvest[36]—wondering if maybe old Teofilo was actually at sheep camp corraling[37] the sheep for the night. But there he was, facing into a cold dry wind and squinting at the last sunlight, ready to bury a red wool blanket while the faces of his parishioners[38] were in shadow with the last warmth of the sun on their backs.

His fingers were stiff, and it took him a long time to twist the lid off the holy water. Drops of water fell on the red blanket and soaked into dark icy spots. He sprinkled the grave and the water disappeared almost before it touched the dim, cold sand; it reminded him of something—he tried to remember what it was, because he thought if he could remember he might understand this. He sprinkled more water; he shook the container until it was empty, and the water fell through

28 scuffed: worn and used; not new or polished
29 loafer: casual style of shoe
30 cassock: priest's long robe
31 Christian burial: burial with Christian prayers
32 missionary: person who tries to convince others to adopt a specific religion; some missionaries also try to help people

33 leper: person who has the disease of leprosy
34 pagans: word used by some missionaries to describe people with a different religion
35 perverse: (here) secret and strange
36 harvest: picking food that was planted earlier in the year, such as corn or wheat
37 corraling: gathering the sheep together
38 parishioners: members of a church under the leadership of a priest or a minister

the light from sundown like August rain that fell while the sun was still shining, almost evaporating[39] before it touched the wilted squash flowers.

   The wind pulled at the priest's brown Franciscan robe and swirled away the corn meal and pollen that had been sprinkled on the blanket. They lowered the bundle into the ground, and they didn't bother to untie the stiff pieces of new rope that were tied around the ends of the blanket. The sun was gone, and over on the highway the eastbound lane[40] was full of headlights. The priest walked away slowly. Leon watched him climb the hill, and when he had disappeared within the tall, thick walls, Leon turned to look up at the high blue mountains in the deep snow that reflected a faint red light from the west. He felt good because it was finished, and he was happy about the sprinkling of the holy water; now the old man could send them big thunderclouds for sure.[41]

130

39 evaporating: liquid, such as water, becoming part of the air
40 eastbound lane: the side of the road with cars going east
41 for sure: definitely; certainly

Understanding the Story

Working individually or in small groups, retell the story in this chapter by filling in the blanks in the following sentences.

1. In this story, Leon and Ken found Grandfather (Teofilo) under a big _____. They didn't have any trouble finding him because his jacket and pants were _____. Because the weather was very _____ for this time of year, Leon _____ his jacket.

2. Leon took a piece of string out of his pocket and _____ a small gray feather in the old man's _____. Ken gave Leon some paint. Leon _____ a streak of white across Grandfather's forehead, and a strip of _____ along the high _____.

3. Then Ken threw pinches of _____ and _____ into the wind. Leon painted yellow under the old man's _____ and _____ across his chin. Next, Ken said, "_____."

4. Leon and Ken put Grandfather's body in the back of the _____ and then _____ the bundle with a heavy tarp. As Leon and Ken were driving home, they saw the car of Father Paul. The priest _____ his hand for them to stop.

5. The priest asked Leon and Ken if they had found Teofilo. Leon and Ken told him _____.

6. When Leon and Ken got home, they explained to _____ and _____ what happened at the sheep camp. Then they dressed Grandfather in _____ clothes. Ken left to find the people who would dig the _____. Neighbors and relatives come to the house because they wanted to _____ and _____.

7. At the Indian funeral, Louise _____ corn meal around the old man. She told Leon it would be a good idea to ask the priest to _____ so that Grandfather

_____.

8. Leon and Ken went to ask the priest to bring holy water to _____. The priest said Leon and Ken should have _____ so that he could bring the Last Rites. Leon told the priest _____.

9. The priest went with Leon and Ken to the graveyard. Because it was late in the day, they could see only half of the _____ as it was sinking in the west. It was the month of _____, the end of winter, so the priest thought the _____ would be frozen. But they were in the state of _____, in the southwest United States, so the ground was sand and not frozen.

10. When the priest looked at the small red blanket containing Grandfather, he wondered _____. Then the priest _____. Leon was glad because

_____.

Talking and Writing

With your classmates, use these questions as starting points for discussion of ideas presented in the story. Then select a question and write an essay on the topic.

1. How does the author use the following incidents to show that the Indians and Father Paul see things differently?
  • Father Paul and the Indians see each other on the road, after Leon and Ken find Grandfather. (Why do you think Leon and Ken didn't tell the priest that Grandfather is dead?)
  • Leon and Ken ask Father Paul for holy water. (How does Father Paul feel about the request?)
  • Father Paul brings holy water to the grave. (Why does the priest doubt that the Indians are burying Grandfather?)

2. How would you summarize this story from the point of view of Father Paul? How do you think he feels about his relationship with the Indians? How do you think he feels about the way the Indians see life?

Why do you think the priest has difficulty understanding or accepting the point of view of the Indians?

3. Why did Leon and Ken ask the priest to sprinkle holy water? (Why did the priest want to sprinkle holy water?)

How have the modern Indians in this story combined the Indian culture with the white man's culture?

4. How is the Indian attitude toward death presented in this story? Are the Indians afraid of death? What did Leon and Ken do when they found Grandfather? (How does this attitude contrast with the attitudes of other cultures toward death?)

5. In the next to last paragraph of the story, the author describes how the holy water looked when the priest sprinkled it on the grave. Why do you think the author includes this image in the story?

6. Do you know of other countries where descendants of the original inhabitants still live? What are the conditions of their lives and how have their cultures continued? How have the new and old cultures mixed?

What is the attitude of other people in those countries toward the original inhabitants? How are these native peoples usually described in movies and books?

7. What can be done to prevent cultures from dying out? How do we keep languages and traditions from disappearing?

What are the advantages of living apart from other cultures, such as on a reservation? What are the disadvantages?

More Ideas

1. Libraries and bookstores have books about the lives of native Americans and native Canadians today.

You can also check with your local library, or check the phone book, for the names of Indian organizations that can provide you with information about Indian tribes nearly. Schools or your local government may also have information about Indian groups.

"The Man to Send Rain Clouds" is the title story in a collection of stories by native American writers (*The Man to Send Rainclouds*, edited by Kenneth Rosen). Another collection of stories by American Indians is *Earth Power Coming*, edited by Simon Ortiz.

Suggested fictional reading by American Indian writers: *The Way to Rainy Mountain* by N. Scott Momaday; *Love Medicine* by Louise Erdrich; *A Yellow Raft in Blue Water* by Michael Dorris.

Suggested fictional reading by Canadian Indian writers: *Moose Meat and Wild Rice* by Basil Johnston; *The Rez Sisters* by Tomson Highway.

All My Relations: An Anthology of Contemporary Canadian Native Fiction is edited by Thomas King and includes writing by Peter Blue Cloud, Tomson Highway, Jeannette Armstrong, and Basil Johnston.

Suggested nonfiction and historical readings about American Indians: *Bury My Heart at Wounded Knee* by Dee Brown; *Black Elk Speaks* as told through John G. Neihardt; *In the Spirit of Crazy Horse* by Peter Matthiessen; *Black Elk: The Sacred Ways of a Lakota* by Wallace Black Elk and William S. Lyon.

Suggested nonfiction and historical readings about Canadian Indians: *First People, First Voices*, edited by Penny Petrone; *Chief: The Fearless Vision of Billy Diamond* by Roy MacGregor; *Prison Stronger than Love: The Destruction of an Ojibway Community* by Anastasia Shkilnyk; and *Indian School Days* by Basil Johnston.

2. You may have already heard some of the terms and names in the following list. Take one of the words listed and find out what it describes. Explain the word briefly to your class, or write a short paper.

Wounded Knee	Geronimo
Crazy Horse	pow-wow
medicine man	teepee
buffalo	treaty
Battle of Little Big Horn (Custer's Last Stand)	hunting grounds

3. Describe the daily life and customs of a specific Indian nation or tribe, such as the Indians near where you live.

Or you could tell about a legend or a tradition of this group, or how their culture has changed.

For example, libraries and bookstores will have information about the Cree, Ojibway, and Dene Indians in Canada; the Shoshone in western United States; the Cheyenne, Nez Perce, Dakota, and Osage in the Great Plains; the Hopi, Navajo, Comanche, and Apache in the southwest United States; the Seminole and Natchez

Indians in the southeast; and the Iroquois, Algonquin, and Delaware Indians in the eastern United States.

You could find out about the Iroquois Confederation of the Five Nations: the Mohawk, Oneida, Seneca, Cayuga, and the Onondaga. Who was Dekanawidah? What was the Iroquois constitution?

4. Find out about the original inhabitants of a country in another part of the world and write a short paper or give a brief talk to your class.

    For example, you could talk about the Maya or the Aztec Indians, the Incas in Peru, the Australian aborigines, or the Maoris in New Zealand. (If you have a book with photos, bring it to class.)

    Describe an aspect of their culture, such as their art or one of their traditional stories. What are the roles of children and old people in their society?

5. "The Man to Send Rainclouds" takes place in New Mexico. At the grave, the priest notices that the land is all sand. Find out what the American Southwest looks like and write a paper on the topic, or give a short talk to the class. Which plants and trees grow there? Which animals live there? (Bring books with photos to class, if you can.)

Building Vocabulary

1. You can often get a general idea of a word's meaning by looking at the sentence or paragraph in which it appears.

    Take a look at the *italicized* words in the following sentences and guess what each one means. Then check your dictionary to get an exact meaning of each word and see if your guess was correct.

    a) At the beginning of the story, Ken came *sliding* down the river bank, carrying a red blanket.

       Sliding probably means:

    b) When Father Paul went with Ken to sprinkle the holy water at Grandfather's grave, both men had to *stoop* to fit through the low entrance.

       Stoop probably means:

    c) At the end of the story, there were many *headlights* in the eastbound land of the highway.

                    Headlights probably means:

2. Each of the following words from the story has at least two meanings. How is each word used in the story? Check your English-English dictionary for other meanings for these words.

    pen   bank   loafer   wave

3. Complete the following sentences, using the appropriate words from this list. Be sure to use the correct form of each word.

    fade   wander   evaporate   brother-in-law

    a) Your husband's brother is your _____.

    b) After Grandfather died, the sheep _____ all over the arroyo.

    c) Your sister's husband is your _____.

    d) Grandfather's jacket and pants were _____ from being exposed to the sun.

    e) Your wife's brother is your _____.

    f) When the priest sprinkled the holy water at Grandfather's grave, it seemed to be almost _____ before it reached the ground.

And Sarah Laughed

Joanne Greenberg

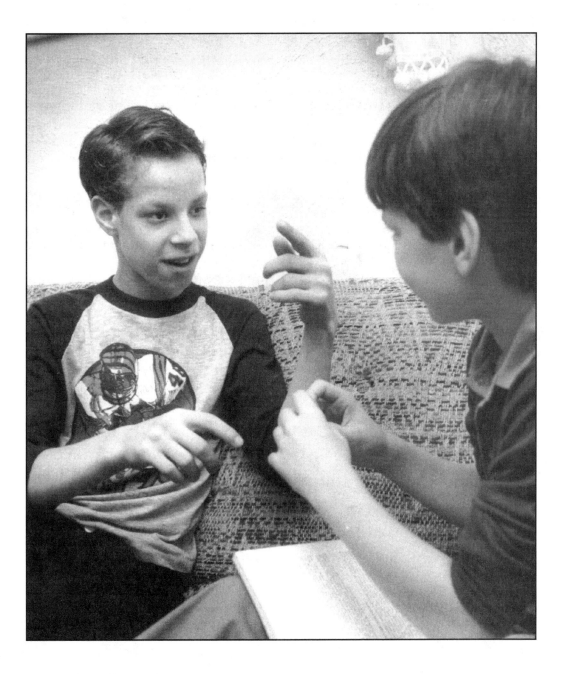

Before You Begin . . .

In the same way that hearing people use spoken languages such as English, Spanish, and Japanese to express themselves, deaf people all over the world use sign languages to communicate.

Instead of using sounds, sign languages use specific hand movements and hand positions in complex ways. Each system of sign language is different; for example, deaf people who use Italian Sign Language do not easily understand those who use Chinese Sign Language.

American Sign Language (ASL or Ameslan) is the sign language used most often in the United States and Canada, with variations used in different regions of North America. In the Canadian province of Quebec, which is primarily French-speaking, LSQ is used (*la Langue des Signes de Québecois*).

However, languages used by the deaf are not imitations of spoken languages. In fact, sign languages have their own vocabulary and grammar.

Born in New York in 1932, Joanne Greenberg now lives in Colorado. The topics of Greenberg's books and short stories are varied: In addition to writing about the lives of the deaf, she has written about bigotry in twelfth-century England and about a schizophrenic teenager's recovery from mental illness.

Before reading this story, your class could briefly discuss your impressions of how deafness affects people's lives. Have you ever known people who are deaf? How do they communicate with each other and with hearing people? What kind of work do they do?

You might want to read the story twice: once for meaning, and again to pick up more vocabulary and understand the story better.

To practice using some of the vocabulary in this story, take a look at the section "Building Vocabulary" at the end of the chapter.

And Sarah Laughed

Joanne Greenberg

She went to the window every fifteen minutes to see if they were coming. They would be taking the new highway cutoff; it would bring them past the south side of the farm; past the unused, dilapidated[1] outbuildings instead of the orchards[2] and fields that were now full and green. It would look like a poor place to the new bride.[3] Her first impression of their farm would be of age and bleached-out,[4] dried-out buildings on which the doors hung open like a row of gaping mouths that said nothing.

All day, Sarah had gone about her work clumsy with eagerness and hesitant with dread,[5] picking up utensils to forget them in holding, finding them two minutes later a surprise in her hand. She had been planning and working ever since Abel wrote to them from Chicago that he was coming home with a wife. Everything should have been clean and orderly. She wanted the bride to know as soon as she walked inside what kind of woman Abel's mother was—to feel, without a word having to be said, the house's dignity, honesty, simplicity, and love. But the spring cleaning had been late, and Alma Yoder had gotten sick— Sarah had had to go over to the Yoders and help out.

Now she looked around and saw that it was no use trying[6] to have everything ready in time. Abel and his bride would be coming any minute. If she didn't want to get caught shedding tears of frustration, she'd better get herself under control. She stepped over the pile of clothes still unsorted for the laundry and went out on the back porch.

The sky was blue and silent, but as she watched, a bird passed over the fields crying. The garden spread out before her, displaying its varying greens. Beyond it, along the creek, there was a row of poplars.[7] It always calmed her to look at them. She looked today. She and Matthew had planted those trees. They stood thirty feet high now, stately as figures in a procession. Once—only once and many years ago—she had tried to describe in words the sounds that the wind made as it combed those trees on its way west. The little boy to whom she had spoken was a grown man now, and he was bringing home a wife. *Married* . . .

Ever since he had written to tell them he was coming with his bride, Sarah had been going back in her mind to the days when she and Matthew were bride and groom and then mother and father. Until now, it hadn't seemed so long ago.

1 **dilapidated:** old and needing repair
2 **orchard:** group of fruit trees
3 **bride:** recently married woman
4 **bleached-out:** (here) color faded from the sun
5 **dread:** fear; anxiety about what's going to happen

6 **it was no use trying:** there was no reason to try because it couldn't be done
7 **poplar:** kind of tree that's tall and thin

Her life had flowed on past her, blurring the early days with Matthew when this farm was strange and new to her and when the silence of it was sharp and bitter like pain, not dulled and familiar like an echo of old age.

Matthew hadn't changed much. He was a tall, lean man, but he had had a boy's spareness[8] then. She remembered how his smile came, wavered and went uncertainly, but how his eyes had never left her. He followed everything with his eyes. Matthew had always been a silent man; his face was expressionless and his
40   body stiff with reticence,[9] but his eyes had sought her out eagerly and held her and she had been warm in his look.

Sarah and Matthew had always known each other—their families had been neighbors. Sarah was a plain[10] girl, a serious "decent" girl.[11] Not many of the young men asked her out, and when Matthew did and did again, her parents had been pleased. Her father told her that Matthew was a good man, as steady[12] as any woman could want. He came from honest, hard-working people and he would prosper any farm he had.[13] Her mother spoke shyly of how his eyes woke when Sarah came into the room, and how they followed her. If she married him, her life would be full of the things she knew and loved, an easy, familiar world with her
50   parents' farm not two miles down the road. But no one wanted to mention the one thing that worried Sarah: the fact that Matthew was deaf. It was what stopped her from saying yes right away; she loved him, but she was worried about his deafness. The things she feared about it were the practical things: a fall or a fire when he wouldn't hear her cry for help. Only long after she had put those fears aside and moved the scant two miles[14] into his different world, did she realize that the things she had feared were the wrong things.

Now they had been married for twenty-five years. It was a good marriage—good enough. Matthew was generous, strong, and loving. The farm prospered. His silence made him seem more patient, and because she became more silent
60   also, their neighbors saw in them the dignity and strength of two people who do not rail against misfortune,[15] who were beyond[16] trivial talk and gossip; whose lives needed no words. Over the years of help given and meetings attended, people noticed how little they needed to say. Only Sarah's friend Luita knew that in the beginning, when they were first married, they had written yearning[17] notes to each other. But Luita didn't know that the notes also were mute.[18] Sarah had never shown them to anyone, although she kept them all, and sometimes she

---

8 spareness: thinness
9 reticence: hesitant or quiet nature
10 plain: (here) not pretty, not ugly
11 serious "decent" girl: (here) girl who's polite and from a family with a good reputation
12 steady: reliable; something you can count on
13 would prosper any farm he had: would make a farm financially strong

14 scant two miles: slightly less than two miles
15 rail against misfortune: complain strongly and bitterly about bad luck
16 were beyond: (here) had more important things to do
17 yearning: deep desire
18 mute: silent

would go up and get the box out of her closet and read them over. She had saved every scrap,[19] from questions about the eggs to the tattered note he had left beside his plate on their first anniversary. He had written it when she was busy at the stove and then he'd gone out and she hadn't seen it until she cleared the table. **70**

The note said: "I love you derest wife Sarah. I pray you have happy day all day your life."[20]

When she wanted to tell him something, she spoke to him slowly, facing him, and he took the words as they formed on her lips. His speaking voice was thick and hard to understand and he perceived that it was unpleasant. He didn't like to use it. When he had to say something, he used his odd, grunting tone, and she came to understand what he said. If she ever hungered for laughter from him or the little meaningless talk that confirms[21] existence and affection, she told herself angrily that Matthew talked through his work. Words die in the air; they can be turned one way or another, but Matthew's work prayed and laughed for him. He **80** took good care of her and the boys, and they idolized[22] him. Surely that counted more than all the words—words that meant and didn't mean—behind which people could hide.

Over the years she seldom noticed her own increasing silence, and there were times when his tenderness,[23] which was always given without words, seemed to her to make his silence beautiful.

She thought of the morning she had come downstairs feeling heavy and off balance with her first pregnancy—with Abel. She had gone to the kitchen to begin the day, taking the coffeepot down and beginning to fill it when her eye caught something on the kitchen table. For a minute she looked around in **90** confusion. They had already laid away[24] what the baby would need: diapers, little shirts and bedding, all folded away in the drawer upstairs, but here on the table was a bounty of cloth, all planned and scrimped[25] for and bought from careful, careful study of the catalogue[26]—yards of patterned flannel[27] and plissé, coat wool, and bright red corduroy. Sixteen yards of yellow ribbon for bindings. Under the coat wool was cloth Matthew had chosen for her; blue with a little gray figure. It was silk, and there was a card on which was rolled precisely enough lace edging for her collar and sleeves. All the long studying and careful planning, all in silence.

She had run upstairs and thanked him and hugged him, but it was no use **100** showing delight with words, making plans, matching cloth and figuring which

---

19 scrap: small piece
20 "I pray you have happy day all day your life": When Matthew expresses himself in English, his sentence constructions reflect his own interpretation of language. Although Matthew can read, he can't listen to the ways hearing people construct sentences in English.
21 confirms: supports that something is true

22 idolized: admired as though he were a god
23 tenderness: gentleness; expression of love
24 laid away: prepared and saved for later use
25 scrimped: carefully saved money
26 catalogue: (here) a book listing items that can be bought through the mail
27 flannel: type of soft cotton or wool

pieces would be for the jacket and which for sleepers. Most wives used such fussing to tell their husbands how much they thought of their gifts. But Matthew's silence was her silence too.

When he had left to go to the orchard after breakfast that morning, she had gone to their room and stuffed her ears with cotton, trying to understand the world as it must be to him, with no sound. The cotton dulled the outside noises a little, but it only magnified[28] all the noises in her head. Scratching her cheek caused a roar[29] like a downpour of rain; her own voice was like thunder. She knew Matthew could not hear his own voice in his head. She could not be deaf as he was deaf. She could not know such silence ever.

So she found herself talking to the baby inside her, telling it the things she would have told Matthew, the idle daily things: Didn't Margaret Amson look peaked[30] in town? Wasn't it a shame the drugstore had stopped stocking[31] lump alum—her pickles wouldn't be the same.

Abel was a good baby. He had Matthew's great eyes and gentle ways. She chattered[32] to him all day, looking forward to his growing up, when there would be confidences between them. She looked to the time when he would have his own picture of the world, and with that keen hunger and hope she had a kind of late blooming[33] into a beauty that made people in town turn to look at her when she passed in the street holding the baby in the fine clothes she had made for him. She took Abel everywhere, and came to know a pride that was very new to her, a plain girl from a modest family who had married a neighbor boy. When they went to town, they always stopped over to see Matthew's parents and her mother.

Mama had moved to town after Pa died. Of course they had offered to have Mama come and live with them, but Sarah was glad she had gone to a little place in town, living where there were people she knew and things happening right outside her door. Sarah remembered them visiting on a certain spring day, all sitting in Mama's new front room. They sat uncomfortably in the genteel chairs, and Abel crawled around on the floor as the women talked, looking up every now and then for his father's nod of approval. After a while he went to catch the sunlight that was glancing off a crystal nut dish and scattering rainbow bands[34] on the floor. Sarah smiled down at him. She too had a radiance,[35] and, for the first time in her life, she knew it. She was wearing the dress she had made from Matthew's cloth—it became her[36] and she knew that too, so she gave her joy freely as she traded news with Mama.

---

28 **magnified:** made larger
29 **roar:** very loud, deep sound such as a lion makes
30 **peaked:** (here) tired or sick
31 **stocking:** (here) selling in the store
32 **chattered:** (here) talked rapidly without stopping

33 **blooming:** time when a flower opens up
34 **glancing off a crystal . . . rainbow bands:** the glass dish was breaking the light into many colors
35 **radiance:** (here) beauty from happiness
36 **became her:** (here) made her look pretty

Suddenly they heard the fire bell[37] ringing up on the hill. She caught Matthew's eye and mouthed, "Fire engines," pointing uphill to the firehouse. He nodded.

In the next minutes there was the strident, off-key blare[38] as every single one   **140** of Arcadia's volunteer firemen—his car horn plugged with a matchstick and his duty before him—drove hell-bent for the firehouse in an ecstasy[39] of bell and siren. In a minute the ding-ding-ding-ding[40] careened in deafening,[41] happy privilege through every red light in town.

"Big bunch of boys!" Mama laughed. "You can count two Saturdays in good weather when they don't have a fire, and that's during the hunting season!"

They laughed. Then Sarah looked down at Abel, who was still trying to catch the wonderful colors. A madhouse[42] of bells, horns, screaming sirens had gone right past them and he hadn't cried, he hadn't looked, he hadn't turned. Sarah twisted her head sharply away and screamed to the china cats on the whatnot   **150** shelf[43] as loud as she could, but Abel's eyes only flickered to the movement and then went back to the sun and its colors.

Mama whispered, "Oh, my dear God!"

Sarah began to cry bitterly, uncontrollably, while her husband and son looked on, confused, embarrassed, unknowing.

The silence drew itself over the seasons and the seasons layered into years. Abel was a good boy; Matthew was a good man.

Later, Rutherford, Lindsay, and Franklin Delano[44] came. They too were silent. Hereditary nerve deafness was rare,[45] the doctors all said. The boys might marry and produce deaf children, but it was not likely. When they started to school, the   **160** administrators and teachers told her that the boys would be taught specially to read lips and to speak. They would not be "abnormal,"[46] she was told. Nothing would show their handicap,[47] and with training no one need know that they were deaf. But the boys seldom used their lifeless voices[48] to call to their friends; they seldom joined games unless they were forced to join. No one but their mother understood their speech. No teacher could stop all the jumping, turning, gum-chewing schoolboys, or remember herself to face front from the blackboard to the

---

37 fire bell: bell that tells the community of a fire
38 strident, off-key blare: sound that's very loud and not at all musical
39 ecstasy: great happiness
40 ding-ding-ding-ding: sound of the fire bell
41 deafening: so loud it could make you deaf
42 madhouse: (here) lots of confusion and disorder. The adjective *mad* can mean either *angry* or *insane*, and *madhouse* is an old term for an institution for the mentally ill.
43 whatnot shelf: shelf holding miscellaneous decorations
44 Franklin Delano: Franklin Delano

Roosevelt (FDR) was a popular president during the years of the Depression (the 1930s) and during World War II (the early 1940s)
45 hereditary nerve deafness was rare: deaf parents do not usually pass deafness on to their children
46 "abnormal": not normal; Sarah is quoting the exact word they used
47 handicap: disadvantage, something missing
48 lifeless voices: voices without emotion. Because deaf people don't hear themselves or others speak, they can't easily imitate how a voice sounds.

sound-closed boys. The lip-reading exercises[49] never seemed to make plain differences—"man," "pan," "began."

170   But the boys had work and pride in the farm. The seasons varied their silence with colors—crows[50] flocked in the snowy fields in winter, and tones of golden wheat darkened across acres of summer wind. If the boys couldn't hear the bedsheets flapping on the washline, they could see and feel the autumn day. There were chores and holidays and the wheel of birth and planting, hunting, fishing, and harvest. The boys were familiar in town; nobody ever laughed at them, and when Sarah met neighbors at the store, they praised her sons with exaggerated praise, well meant,[51] saying that no one could tell, no one could really tell unless they knew, about the boys not hearing.

Sarah wanted to cry to these kindly women that the simple orders the boys
180   obeyed by reading her lips were not a miracle. If she could ever hear in their long-practiced robot voices a question that had to do with feelings and not facts, and answer it in words that rose beyond the daily, tangible[52] things done or not done, *that* would be a miracle.

Her neighbors didn't know that they themselves confided to one another from a universe of hopes, a world they wanted half lost in the world that was; how often they spoke pitting inflection against meaning[53] to soften it, harden it, make a joke of it, curse by it, bless by it. They didn't realize how they wrapped the bare words of love in gentle humor or wild insults that the loved ones knew were ways of keeping the secret of love between the speaker and the hearer. Mothers
190   lovingly called their children crow-bait, mouse-meat, devils. They predicted dark ends[54] for them, and the children heard the secrets beneath the words, heard them and smiled and knew, and let the love said-unsaid caress their souls. With her own bitter knowledge Sarah could only thank them for well-meaning and return to silence.

Standing on the back porch now, Sarah heard the wind in the poplars and she sighed. It was getting on to noon. Warm air was beginning to ripple the fields. Matthew would be ready for lunch soon, but she wished she could stand out under the warm sky forever and listen to birds stitching sounds into the endless silence. She found herself thinking about Abel again, and the bride. She
200   wondered what Janice would be like. Abel had gone all the way to Chicago to be trained in drafting.[55] He had met her there, in the school. Sarah was afraid of a girl like that. They had been married quickly, without family or friends or toasts or

---

49 lip-reading exercises: exercises to help deaf children know the difference between words that look the same on the lips. Here, Sarah thinks of how the words *man, pan,* and *began* look the same when they're spoken.
50 crows: large, black birds that make a loud, rough cry
51 well meant: had good intentions but the results weren't good

52 tangible: real; can be felt
53 pitting inflection against meaning: contrasting the tone of the voice to the meaning of the words
54 predicted dark ends: said that bad things would happen in the future
55 drafting: (here) profession involving precise drawing and measuring of buildings or machines

gifts or questions. It hinted[56] at some kind of secret shame. It frightened her. That kind of girl was independent and she might be scornful[57] of a dowdy[58] mother-in-law. And the house was still a mess.

From down the road, dust was rising. Matthew must have seen it, too. He came over the rise and toward the house walking faster than usual. He'd want to slick his hair down and wash up[59] to meet the stranger his son had become. She ran inside and bundled up the unsorted laundry, ran upstairs and pulled a comb through her hair, put on a crooked dab of lipstick, banged her shin,[60] took off her   **210** apron and saw a spot on her dress, put the apron on again and shouted a curse to all the disorder she suddenly saw around her.

Now the car was crunching up the thin gravel[61] of the driveway. She heard Matthew downstairs washing up, not realizing that the bride and groom were already at the house. Protect your own, she thought, and ran down to tell him. Together they went to the door and opened it, hoping that at least Abel's familiar face would comfort them.

They didn't recognize him at first, and he didn't see them. He and the tiny bride might have been alone in the world. He was walking around to open the door for her, helping her out, bringing her up the path to the house, and all the   **220** time their fingers and hands moved and spun meanings at which they smiled and laughed; they were talking somehow, painting thoughts in the air so fast with their fingers that Sarah couldn't see where one began and the other ended. She stared. The school people had always told her that such finger-talk set the deaf apart. It was abnormal; it made freaks of them . . . How soon Abel had accepted someone else's strangeness and bad ways. She felt so dizzy she thought she was going to fall, and she was more bitterly jealous than she had ever been before.

The little bride stopped before them appealingly and in her dead, deaf-rote voice, said, "Ah-am pliizd to meet 'ou."[62] Sarah put out her hand dumbly and it was taken and the girl's eyes shone. Matthew smiled, and this time the girl spoke   **230** and waved her hands in time to her words, and then gave Matthew her hand. So Abel had told that girl about Matthew's deafness. It had never been a secret, but Sarah felt somehow betrayed.

They had lunch, saw the farm, the other boys came home from their summer school and met Janice. Sarah put out cake and tea and showed Abel and Janice up to the room she had made ready for them, and all the time the two of them went on with love-talk in their fingers; the jokes and secrets knitted silently between them, fears told and calmed, hopes spoken and echoed in the silence of a kitchen where twenty-five years of silence had imprisoned her. Always they would stop

---

56 hinted: suggested
57 scornful: felt superior to
58 dowdy: old-fashioned and not sophisticated
59 wash up: wash hands
60 banged her shin: hit the front part of her leg against something

61 thin gravel: small pieces of rock filling the road
62 Ah-am pliizd to meet 'ou: I'm pleased to meet you. Janice's speech is not the same as the speech of a hearing person.

240 and pull themselves back to their good manners, speaking or writing polite questions and answers for the family; but in a moment or two, the talk would flag,[63] the urgent hunger would overcome them and they would fight it, resolutely turning their eyes to Sarah's mouth. Then the signs would creep into their fingers, and the joy of talk into their faces, and they would fall before the conquering need of their communion.[64]

Sarah's friend Luita came the next day, in the afternoon. They sat over tea with the kitchen window open for the cool breeze and Sarah was relieved and grateful to hold to a familiar thing now that her life had suddenly become so strange to her. Luita hadn't changed at all, thank God—not the hand that waved
250 her tea cool or the high giggle that broke into generous laughter.

"She's darling!" Luita said after Janice had been introduced, and, thankfully, had left them. Sarah didn't want to talk about her, so she agreed without enthusiasm.[65]

Luita only smiled back. "Sarah, you'll never pass for pleased[66] with a face like that."

"It's just—just her ways," Sarah said. "She never even wrote to us before the wedding, and now she comes in and—and changes everything. I'll be honest, Luita, I didn't want Abel to marry someone who was deaf. What did we train him for, all those special classes? . . . *not* to marry another deaf person. And she hangs
260 on him like a wood tick[67] all day . . ." She didn't mention the signs. She couldn't.

Luita said, "It's just somebody new in the house, that's all. She's important to you, but a stranger. Addie Purkhard felt the same way and you know what a lovely girl Velma turned out to be. It just took time . . . She's going to have a baby, did she tell you?"

"Baby? Who?" Sarah cried, feeling cold and terrified.

"Why, *Velma*. A baby due about a month after my Dolores'."

It had never occurred to Sarah that Janice and Abel could have a baby. She wanted to stop thinking about it and she looked back at Luita whose eyes were glowing with something joyful that had to be said. Luita hadn't been able to see
270 beyond it to the anguish[68] of her friend.

Luita said, "You know, Sarah, things haven't been so good between Sam and me. . . ." She cleared her throat. "You know how stubborn[69] he is. The last few weeks, it's been like a whole new start for us. I came over to tell you about it because I'm so happy, and I had to share it with you."

She looked away shyly, and Sarah pulled herself together and leaned forward, putting her hand on her friend's arm. "I'm so happy for you. What happened?"

---

63 flag: (here) slow down or stop from lack of interest
64 communion: shared thoughts and feelings
65 enthusiasm: intense positive feeling
66 you'll never pass for pleased: you'll never be able to convince people you're happy
67 tick: small insect that attaches itself to the skin of animals or humans
68 anguish: emotional pain
69 stubborn: won't change his or her mind

"It started about three weeks ago—a night that neither of us could get to sleep. We hadn't been arguing; there was just that awful coldness, as if we'd both been frozen stiff. One of us started talking—just lying there in the dark. I don't even know who started, but pretty soon we were telling each other the most secret **280** things—things we never could have said in the light. He finally told me that Dolores having a baby makes him feel old and scared. He's afraid of it, Sarah, and I never knew it, and it explains why he hates to go over and see them, and why he argues with Ken all the time. Right there beside me he told me so many things I'd forgotten or misunderstood. In the dark it's like thinking out loud—like being alone and yet together at the same time. I love him so and I came so close to forgetting it . . ."

Sarah lay in bed and thought about Luita and Sam sharing their secrets in the dark. Maybe even now they were talking in their flower-papered upstairs room, moving against the engulfing seas of silence as if in little boats, finding each **290** other and touching and then looking out in awe[70] at the vastness all around them where they might have rowed alone and mute forever. She wondered if Janice and Abel fingered those signs in the dark on each other's body. She began to cry. There was that freedom, at least; other wives had to strangle their weeping.[71]

When she was cried out, she lay in bed and counted all the good things she had: children, possessions, acres of land, respect of neighbors, the years of certainty and success. Then she conjured the little bride, and saw her standing in front of Abel's old car as she had at first—with nothing; all her virtues[72] still unproven, all her fears still forming, and her bed in another woman's house. Against the new gold ring on the bride's finger, Sarah threw all the substance of **300** her years to weigh for her. The balance went with the bride. It wasn't fair! The balance went with the bride because she had put that communion in the scales[73] as well, and all the thoughts that must have been given and taken between them. It outweighed Sarah's twenty-five years of muteness; outweighed the house and barn and well-tended land, and the sleeping family keeping their silent thoughts.

The days went by. Sarah tortured herself with elaborate courtesy[74] to Janice and politeness to the accomplice[75] son, but she couldn't guard her own envy from herself and she found fault wherever she looked. Now the silence of her house was throbbing with her anger. Every morning Janice would come and ask to help, but Sarah was too restless[76] to teach her, so Janice would sit for a while waiting **310** and then get up and go outside to look for Abel. Then Sarah would decide to make coleslaw[77] and sit with the chopping bowl in her lap, smashing the chopper

---

70 in awe: with deep respect
71 weeping: crying
72 virtues: good qualities
73 scales: an instrument used to compare the weight of two objects, or used to determine how heavy something is
74 tortured herself with elaborate courtesy: made herself miserable by being extremely polite
75 accomplice: assistant in a crime
76 restless: not quiet or relaxed
77 coleslaw: popular kind of salad made of small pieces of cabbage

against the wood with a vindictive joy that she alone could hear the sounds she was making, that she alone knew how savage they were and how satisfying.

At church she would see the younger boys all clean and handsome, Matthew greeting friends, Janice demure and fragile, and Abel proud and loving, and she would feel a terrible guilt for her unreasonable anger; but back from town afterwards, and after Sunday dinner, she noticed as never before how disheveled[78] the boys looked, how ugly their hollow voices sounded. Had Matthew always
320 been so patient and unruffled? He was like one of his own stock,[79] an animal, a dumb animal.

Janice kept asking to help and Sarah kept saying there wasn't time to teach her. She was amazed when Matthew, who was very fussy about his fruit, suggested to her that Janice might be able to take care of the grapes and, later, work in the orchard.

"I haven't time to teach her!"

"Ah owill teeech Ja-nuss," Abel said, and they left right after dinner in too much of a hurry.

Matthew stopped Sarah when she was clearing the table and asked why she
330 didn't like Janice. Now it was Sarah's turn to be silent, and when Matthew insisted, Sarah finally turned on him. "You don't understand," she shouted. "You don't understand a thing!" And she saw on his face the same look of confusion she had seen that day in Mama's fussy front room when she had suddenly begun to cry and could not stop. She turned away with the plates, but suddenly his hand shot out and he struck them to the floor, and the voice he couldn't hear or control rose to an awful cry, "Ah ahm dehf! Ah ahm dehf!" Then he went out, slamming the door[80] without the satisfaction of its sound.

If a leaf fell or a stalk sprouted in the grape arbor, Janice told it over like a set of prayers. One night at supper, Sarah saw the younger boys framing those dumb-
340 signs of hers, and she took them outside and slapped their hands, "*We* don't do that!" she shouted at them, and to Janice later she said, "Those . . . signs you make—I know they must have taught you to do that, but out here—well, it isn't our way."

Janice looked back at her in a confusion for which there were no words.

It was no use raging[81] at Janice. Before she had come there had never been anything for Sarah to be angry about . . . What did they all expect of her? Wasn't it enough that she was left out of a world that heard and laughed without being humiliated[82] by the love-madness they made with their hands? It was like watching them undressing.

350   The wind cannot be caught. Poplars may sift it, a rising bird can breast it, but

---

78 disheveled: dressed in a way that's messy and disorganized
79 stock: (here) animals on a farm
80 slamming the door: shutting the door loudly, with force
81 raging: expressing a lot of anger
82 humiliated: extremely embarrassed

it will pass by and no one can stop it. She saw the boys coming home at a dead run now,[83] and they couldn't keep their hands from taking letters, words, and pictures from the fingers of the lovers. If they saw an eagle, caught a fish, or got scolded, they ran to their brother or his wife, and Sarah had to stand in the background and demand to be told.

One day Matthew came up to her and smiled and said, "Look." He put out his two index fingers and hooked the right down on the left, then the left down gently on the right. "Fwren,"[84] he said, "Ja-nuss say, fwren."

To Sarah there was something obscene[85] about all those gestures, and she said, "I don't like people waving their hands around like monkeys in a zoo!" She said **360** it very clearly so that he couldn't mistake it.

He shook his head violently and gestured as he spoke. "Mouth eat; mouth kiss, mouth tawk! Fin-ger wohk; fin-ger tawk. E-ah" (and he grabbed his ear, violently), "e-ah dehf. *Mihn*," (and he rapped his head, violently, as if turning a terrible impatience against himself so as to spare her) "*mihn not* dehf!"

Later she went to the barn after something and she ran into Lindsay and Franklin Delano standing guiltily, and when she caught them in her eye as she turned, she saw their hands framing signs. They didn't come into the house until it was nearly dark. Was their hunger for those signs so great that only darkness could bring them home? They weren't bad boys, the kind who would do a thing **370** just because you told them not to. Did their days have a hunger too, or was it only the spell of the lovers, honey-honeying to shut out a world of moving mouths and silence?

At supper she looked around the table and was reassured. It could have been any farm family sitting there, respectable and quiet. A glance from the father was all that was needed to keep order or summon another helping. Their eyes were lowered, their faces composed. The hands were quiet. She smiled and went to the kitchen to fix the shortcake she had made as a surprise.

When she came back, they did not notice her immediately. They were all busy talking. Janice was telling them something and they all had their mouths **380** ridiculously pursed with the word. Janice smiled in assent[86] and each one showed her his sign and she smiled at each one and nodded, and the signers turned to one another in their joy, accepting and begging acceptance. Then they saw Sarah standing there; the hands came down, the faces faded.

She took the dinner plates away and brought in the dessert things, and when she went back to the kitchen for the cake, she began to cry. It was beyond envy[87] now; it was too late for measuring or weighing. She had lost. In the country of the blind, Mama used to say, the one-eyed man is king. Having been a citizen of such

---

83 at a dead run: as quickly as they could
84 Fwren: friend. Matthew is teaching Sarah how to move her fingers to make the sign for *friend.*

85 obscene: offensive to society's standards of decent behavior
86 in assent: in agreement
87 envy: desire for something that belongs to someone else

a country, she knew better. In the country of the deaf, the hearing man is lonely.
390   Into that country a girl had come who, with a wave of her hand, had given the
deaf ears for one another, and had made Sarah the deaf one.

Sarah stood, staring at her cake and feeling for that moment the profundity[88]
of the silence which she had once tried to match by stuffing cotton in her ears.
Everyone she loved was in the other room, talking, sharing, standing before the
awful, impersonal heaven and the unhearing earth with pictures of his thoughts,
and she was the deaf one now. It wasn't "any farm family," silent in its strength.
It was a yearning family, silent in its hunger, and a demure little bride had shown
them all how deep the hunger was. She had shown Sarah that her youth had been
sold into silence. She was too old to change now.

400   An anger rose in her as she stared at the cake. Why should they be free to
move and gesture and look different while she was kept in bondage[89] to their
silence? Then she remembered Matthew's mute notes, his pride in Abel's
training, his face when he had cried, "I am deaf!" over and over. She had actually
fought that terrible yearning, that hunger they all must have had for their own
words. If they could all speak somehow, what would the boys tell her?

She knew what she wanted to tell them. That the wind sounds through the
poplar trees, and people have a hard time speaking to one another even if they
aren't deaf. Luita and Sam had to have a night to hide their faces while they
spoke. It suddenly occurred to her that if Matthew made one of those signs with
410   his hands and she could learn that sign, she could put her hands against his in the
darkness, and read the meaning—that if she learned those signs she could hear
him . . .

She dried her eyes hurriedly and took in the cake. They saw her and the hands
stopped, drooping[90] lifelessly again; the faces waited mutely. Silence. It was a
silence she could no longer bear. She looked from face to face. What was behind
those eyes she loved? Didn't everyone's world go deeper than chores and bread
and sleep?

"I want to talk to you," she said. "I want to talk, to know what you think."
She put her hands out before her, offering them.

420   Six pair of eyes watched her.

Janice said, "Mo-ther."

Eyes snapped away to Janice; thumb was under lip: the Sign.

Sarah followed them. "Wife," she said, showing her ring.

"Wife," Janice echoed,[91] thumb under lip to the clasp of hands.[92]

Sarah said, "I love . . ."

Janice showed her and she followed hesitantly and then turned to Matthew to
give and to be received in that sign.

---

88 profundity: deepness
89 bondage: slavery
90 drooping: hanging down

91 echoed: repeated
92 clasp of hands: two hands holding each other

Understanding the Story

Work individually or with another student to answer these comprehension questions and review the story's events.

Mark each of the following sentences true or false. If it's true, explain further. If it's false, correct the sentence.

1.____ Sarah and everybody in her family are deaf.

2.____ Sarah was very happy with the cloth Matthew gave her.

3.____ Janice recently married Sarah's oldest boy, Abel.

4.____ Sarah's younger boys learned sign language at school.

5.____ Sarah and Matthew had long talks.

6.____ Sarah wanted to meet Janice.

7.____ Sarah always wanted to learn sign language.

8. What did the neighbors tell Sarah about her boys? What didn't her neighbors understand?

9. What happened that made Luita's relationship with her husband much happier?

10. Sarah tried putting cotton in her ears to find out what it's like to be deaf. What was the result?

Talking and Writing

With your classmates, use these questions as starting points for a discussion of ideas presented in the story. Then select a question and write an essay on the topic.

1. How did Sarah feel when Janice began to teach the boys sign language? Why didn't Sarah want to learn sign language? What finally changed Sarah's mind? What was missing from the lives of the members of this family?

2. Did Sarah have a good life before Janice arrived at the farm? Why or why not? (How did Sarah know Matthew loved her?)

3. Is this an optimistic or a pessimistic story?

4. Why did the school prohibit sign language? How did Matthew and the boys respond to learning sign language? Why would some hearing and deaf people feel that it's better to use lip reading than sign language, while others feel it's more important to use sign language? If you or your child were deaf, which method of communication do you think you would prefer?

5. Describe an experience you've had when you found it difficult to express your feelings in English or another language. How did this problem affect you? What did you do?

6. Imagine you are deaf or blind, or you use a wheelchair. Spend a few minutes planning your daily routine going to work or school.

Then discuss with the rest of the class the adjustments in your life that you would have to make during the day. Be as specific and detailed as possible: Think of each thing you do during the day.

For example, if you are deaf and cannot hear an alarm clock, what would you do to wake up early? If you are blind and cannot see a clock, how will you know when it's time to leave for work? If you cannot walk, how do you get to work? (Would you be able to take this class if you used a wheelchair?)

If many people in the community were deaf, or blind, or using wheelchairs, how do you think the community would adapt to make life easier for people in these groups? Do you think that "in the country of the blind, the one-eyed man is king"?

7. Imagine you are deaf and blind, or you use a wheelchair, and you want to study for a profession.

Write a letter to the school explaining why you would be an excellent student, and what adjustments would need to be made. Or write a letter to an employer explaining why you are the best candidate for a certain job.

Try role-playing with a classmate and have an interview with the school administration or the employer.

More Ideas

1. Discuss with your classmates how deaf people and blind people are treated in different cultures and countries. Do you think society assumes these groups of people are not smart?

What kinds of jobs do the deaf, blind, and physically disabled have in other societies? Are there laws protecting the rights of people in those groups? Have customs or laws changed over the years?

2. What was the sign Matthew taught Sarah that means *friend*? What were the signs Sarah learned at the end of the story? (What did Sarah want to tell Matthew in sign language?)

Libraries, bookstores, and local organizations for the deaf will have information on sign language. You could learn to use a few signs, such as the signs for *hello, please*, and *thank you*, and then teach the rest of the class. Or you could learn to spell your name, using the fingerspelling alphabet.

If you know people who are deaf, you might ask them to teach your class a few signs.

3. Check newspapers and magazines, as well as libraries and bookstores, for books about the lives of deaf people.

Some suggested reading: *Everyone Here Spoke Sign Language: Hereditary Deafness on Martha's Vineyard* by Nora Ellen Groce describes the lives of the deaf in a part of Martha's Vineyard, an island off the coast of Massachusetts. In the eighteenth and nineteenth centuries, there were so many deaf people in that community that the hearing people communicated in sign language as well.

Other books include *In This Sign* by Joanne Greenberg; *The Other Side of Silence* by Arden Neisser; and *Changing the Rules* by Frank Bowe. *When the Mind Hears* by Harlan Lane describes the history of the deaf.

The Story of My Life by Helen Keller describes her life as a deaf and blind person. This story has been made into a movie: *The Miracle Worker*. Another movie about deafness is *Children of a Lesser God*.

4. You could also contact local organizations for the blind to find out about books in Braille and tape recordings for the blind. Schools or the local government may be able to provide information about services for the blind in your community. Local organizations may need volunteers to read books and textbooks on tapes for the blind.

5. Are there any changes you think should be made in society that would improve the lives of the deaf, the blind, or people in wheelchairs?

Would these changes benefit society in any way, or would they simply benefit a few people? Who should pay the cost (family, employer, or government)? Write a letter to a representative of the government expressing your point of view.

Building Vocabulary

1. In this story, the neighbors saw Sarah and Matthew as people who do not complain about their *misfortune*.

   a) What does the prefix *mis* mean? (For example, what do *mistake, misbehave, misconception,* and *misspell* mean?)

   b) What does the word *fortune* mean?

   c) *Misfortune* probably means:

2. What does the prefix *un* mean?

   For example:

   When Janice was at church, she felt guilty because she had such *unreasonable* anger.

   What other words begin with the prefix *un* or end with the suffix *able*?

3. What does the word *less* mean? What does *less* mean when it's a suffix to a word?

   a) Matthew's face was *expressionless*.

   Expressionless probably means:

   b) Sometimes Sarah missed the *meaningless* talk husbands and wives have that makes them feel loved.

   Meaningless probably means:

   c) What other words end in the suffix *less*?

4. Complete the following sentences, using the appropriate words from this list. Be sure to use the correct form of each word.

disorderly   enthusiasm   stubbornness
slammed   catalogued   magnified

a) When you're angry, it can be very satisfying to _____ the door.

b) Sarah had been very busy and hadn't been able to do many of her household chores, so she was upset when she looked at the _____ in her house.

c) A university has descriptions of the courses it offers in a school _____.

d) A special kind of glass you can use to make small things look bigger is called a _____ glass.

e) Sometimes we use different words to describe the same human behavior, depending on who it is we're talking about. For example, we might say, "I am firm. You are _____. He is a pig-headed fool."

f) I really liked studying about astronomy last year, and I'm _____ about taking another course this year.

Los Angeles Notebook

Joan Didion

Before You Begin . . .

When we think of Los Angeles, we think first of Hollywood, where movies are made, and we think of young people surfing on the waves of the Pacific Ocean. We also think of smog, of poor air quality in a city that has an extensive system of freeways to handle all the traffic.

Los Angeles is a city of huge neighborhoods, with suburbs covering many miles. It's the financial center for the west coast of the United States; and it's a city with universities, music, and museums—a city with many people of different cultures and nationalities.

In this essay, Joan Didion describes another part of life in Los Angeles, a force of nature that contributes to the city's mood: the Santa Ana wind.

When this hot, dry wind blows, says the author, it has a direct effect on the behavior of the people who live in and around Los Angeles. The Santa Ana wind only happens a few times a year, but people can sense its presence even before it arrives.

Born in 1934 in the Sacramento Valley to a family that had settled in California in the nineteenth century, Didion is best known for writing that describes points of view in and around Los Angeles in southern California, and San Francisco in northern California. This essay appears in Joan Didion's collection *Slouching Towards Bethlehem.*

Before reading this essay, you could be thinking about unusual weather you've seen. For example, has someone in your class been in an earthquake or a hurricane?

For a summary of the author's ideas, see the exercises in the section "Understanding the Essay" after the essay.

To practice using some of the vocabulary, take a look at the section "Building Vocabulary," at the end of the chapter.

Of the many cultures in Los Angeles, one of the most prominent is the Mexican-American (Chicano) culture. Many people in the area speak Spanish.

And many of the names in southern California reflect Spain's early exploration and control of the area. In the late eighteenth century, the Spanish gave the town its name: *El Pueblo de Nuestra Señora la Reina de Los Angeles* (The City of Our Lady Queen of the Angels).

Sometimes the city is referred to by its translation from Spanish: City of Angels.

Los Angeles Notebook

Joan Didion

There is something uneasy[1] in the Los Angeles air this afternoon, some unnatural stillness, some tension. What it means is that tonight a Santa Ana will begin to blow, a hot wind from the northeast whining[2] down through the Cajon and San Gorgonio Passes,[3] blowing up sandstorms[4] out along Route 66,[5] drying the hills and the nerves to the flash point. For a few days now we will see smoke back in the canyons,[6] and hear sirens[7] in the night. I have neither heard nor read that a Santa Ana is due,[8] but I know it, and almost everyone I have seen today knows it too. We know it because we feel it. The baby frets.[9] The maid sulks. I rekindle a waning argument[10] with the telephone company, then cut my losses[11] and lie down, given over to whatever it is in the air. **10** To live with the Santa Ana is to accept, consciously or unconsciously, a deeply mechanistic[12] view of human behavior.

I recall being told, when I first moved to Los Angeles and was living on an isolated beach, that the Indians would throw themselves into the sea when the bad wind blew. I could see why. The Pacific turned ominously[13] glossy[14] during a Santa Ana period, and one woke in the night[15] troubled not only by the peacocks[16] screaming in the olive trees but by the eerie absence of surf.[17] The heat was surreal.[18] The sky had a yellow cast, the kind of light sometimes called "earthquake weather." My only neighbor would not come out of her house for days, and there were no lights at night, and her husband roamed the place[19] with a **20** machete.[20] One day he would tell me that he had heard a trespasser,[21] the next a

---

1 something uneasy: uncomfortable feeling that something bad is going to happen
2 whining: sounding like an irritable child
3 Cajon and San Gorgonio Passes: pass is a way through the mountains
4 sandstorms: strong winds carrying sand through the air
5 Route 66: This cross-country road has been replaced by newer highways. A popular song of the 1940s described the highway's route through Missouri, Oklahoma, New Mexico, Arizona, and California: "It winds from Chicago to L.A.—more than two thousand miles all the way."
6 canyon: huge, deep crack in the ground, formed over thousands of years by running water, such as the Grand Canyon in northern Arizona
7 sirens: loud noisemakers used by ambulances, police cars, and fire engines
8 is due: is expected
9 frets: expresses irritation
10 rekindle a waning argument: restarted an argument that was ending
11 cut my losses: stop before I lose more
12 mechanistic: like a machine
13 ominously: in a threatening way
14 glossy: has a smooth, shiny surface
15 one woke in the night: people sometimes woke in the night (here, *one* is used as a pronoun to describe something that could happen to anyone)
16 peacocks: kind of bird with a large tail that can be spread in a fan of many different colors
17 surf: the ocean waves when they break on the shore
18 surreal: dreamlike, unreal quality; surrealism is a 20th century artistic movement, including artists such as Salvador Dali
19 roamed the place: walked around without purpose
20 machete: huge, heavy knife
21 trespasser: someone who wasn't supposed to be on private land

89

rattlesnake.[22]

"On nights like that," Raymond Chandler[23] once wrote about the Santa Ana, "every booze[24] party ends in a fight. Meek[25] little wives feel the edge of the carving knife and study their husbands' necks. Anything can happen." That was the kind of wind it was. I did not know then that there was any basis for the effect it had on all of us, but it turns out to be another of those cases in which science bears out folk wisdom.[26] The Santa Ana, which is named for one of the canyons it rushes through, is a *foehn* wind, like the *foehn* of Austria and Switzerland and the
30 *hamsin* of Israel. There are a number of persistent malevolent[27] winds, perhaps the best known of which are the mistral of France and the Mediterranean sirocco, but a *foehn* wind has distinct characteristics: It occurs on the leeward slope of a mountain range and, although the air begins as a cold mass, it is warmed as it comes down the mountain and appears finally as a hot dry wind. Whenever and wherever a *foehn* blows, doctors hear about headaches and nausea and allergies, about "nervousness," about "depression."[28] In Los Angeles some teachers do not attempt to conduct formal classes during a Santa Ana, because the children become unmanageable. In Switzerland the suicide rate goes up during the *foehn*, and in the courts of some Swiss cantons[29] the wind is considered a mitigating
40 circumstance[30] for crime. Surgeons[31] are said to watch the wind, because blood does not clot[32] normally during a *foehn*. A few years ago an Israeli physicist discovered that not only during such winds, but for the ten or twelve hours which precede[33] them, the air carries an unusually high ratio of positive to negative ions.[34] No one seems to know exactly why that should be; some talk about friction and others suggest solar[35] disturbances. In any case the positive ions are there, and what an excess of positive ions does, in the simplest terms, is make people unhappy. One cannot get much more mechanistic than that.

Easterners[36] commonly complain that there is no "weather" at all in Southern California, that the days and the seasons slip by relentlessly,[37] numbingly bland.[38]
50 That is quite misleading.[39] In fact the climate is characterized by infrequent but violent extremes: two periods of torrential subtropical rains[40] which continue for weeks and wash out the hills and send subdivisions[41] sliding toward the sea; about

---

22 One day he would tell me . . . the next. . .: some days he told me one thing, other days he told me something else (*would* is used here to mean *repeatedly*)
23 Raymond Chandler: mystery writer from the 1930s who wrote about Los Angeles
24 booze: (slang) alcohol
25 meek: timid; quiet
26 folk wisdom: traditional wisdom
27 malevolent: bad; evil
28 "depression": unhappiness; the word is in quotes because the doctors are reporting what the patients said
29 Swiss cantons: states in Switzerland
30 mitigating circumstance: a kind of explanation; an excuse

31 surgeons: doctors who perform operations
32 clot: stop bleeding
33 precede: come before
34 ion: in chemistry, an ion is an electrically charged atom
35 solar: from the sun
36 Easterners: (here) people who live in the eastern part of the United States
37 relentlessly: without stopping or slowing
38 numbingly bland: so ordinary that it causes lack of feeling
39 misleading: gives the wrong idea
40 torrential subtropical rains: hard, wild rains like those near the tropics
41 subdivision: group of houses in the suburbs

twenty scattered[42] days a year of the Santa Ana, which, with its incendiary[43] dryness, invariably[44] means fire. At the first prediction of a Santa Ana, the Forest Service flies men and equipment from northern California into the southern forests, and the Los Angeles Fire Department cancels its ordinary non-firefighting routines. The Santa Ana caused Malibu to burn the way it did in 1956, and Bel Air in 1961, and Santa Barbara in 1964. In the winter of 1966-67 eleven men were killed fighting a Santa Ana fire that spread through the San Gabriel Mountains. **60**

Just to watch the front-page news out of Los Angeles during a Santa Ana is to get very close to what it is about the place. The longest Santa Ana period in recent years was in 1957, and it lasted not the usual three or four days but fourteen days, from November 21 until December 4. On the first day 25,000 acres of the San Gabriel Mountains were burning, with gusts[45] reaching 100 miles an hour. In town, the wind reached Force 12, or hurricane force, on the Beaufort Scale; oil derricks were toppled[46] and people ordered off the downtown streets to avoid injury from flying objects. On November 22 the fire in the San Gabriels was out of control. On November 24 six people were killed in automobile accidents, and by the end of the week the Los Angeles *Times* was keeping a box **70** score of traffic deaths. On November 26 a prominent Pasadena attorney, depressed about money, shot and killed his wife, their two sons, and himself. On November 27 a South Gate divorcee, twenty-two, was murdered and thrown from a moving car. On November 30 the San Gabriel fire was still out of control, and the wind in town was blowing eighty miles an hour. On the first day of December four people died violently, and on the third the wind began to break.[47]

It is hard for people who have not lived in Los Angeles to realize how radically the Santa Ana figures in the local imagination. The city burning is Los Angeles's deepest image of itself: Nathanael West perceived that, in *The Day of the Locust*; and at the time of the 1965 Watts riots[48] what struck the imagination **80** most indelibly were the fires. For days one could drive the Harbor Freeway and see the city on fire, just as we had always known it would be in the end. Los Angeles weather is the weather of catastrophe,[49] of apocalypse, and, just as the reliably long and bitter winters of New England[50] determine the way life is lived there, so the violence and the unpredictability of the Santa Ana affect the entire quality of life in Los Angeles, accentuate[51] its impermanence,[52] its unreliability. The wind shows us how close to the edge we are.

42 **scattered:** separated
43 **incendiary:** can burn
44 **invariably:** unavoidably
45 **gusts:** violent, sudden winds
46 **oil derricks were toppled:** the tall constructions used to dig oil were knocked over
47 **break:** (here) end
48 **1965 Watts riots:** Watts is a ghetto of black Americans in Los Angeles; frustration, despair,

and anger led some of the residents to burn the neighborhood in 1965
49 **catastrophe:** disaster
50 **New England:** region in the northeast United States, originally a colony of England
51 **accentuate:** highlight; call attention to
52 **impermanence:** lack of permanence

Understanding the Essay

Work individually or with another student to answer these comprehension questions and review the author's points in this essay.

1. The author wrote this essay:
   a) before the Santa Ana wind.
   b) during the Santa Ana wind.
   c) after the wind ended.

2. In Los Angeles, a Santa Ana wind is a hot, dry wind from the:
   a) southeast through the desert.
   b) northeast through the mountains.
   c) west from the ocean.

3. Correct the following:

   The author knows the wind is coming because
   a) the air feels relaxed and pleasant.
   b) the baby sleeps easily.
   c) the author's in a good mood when she talks with the telephone company.

4. When the author first moved to Los Angeles, she was living on a beach with only one other house nearby. What did her neighbor and her neighbor's husband do during periods of the Santa Ana wind?

5. During the Santa Ana wind, how did the area change around the author's isolated beach home?

   a) The Pacific Ocean _____.

   b) The peacocks _____.

   c) The surf _____.

   d) The heat _____.

   e) The sky _____.

6. The Santa Ana wind of Los Angeles is a "foehn" wind, like the foehn of _____ and _____, and the _____ of Israel.

7. During a Santa Ana wind, patients tell their doctors about medical problems such as:

Mark each of the following sentences true or false. If the statement is true, explain further. If it's false, correct the sentence.

8.____ During a Santa Ana wind, some teachers in Los Angeles find the children are easier to teach.

9.____ According to the author, people who don't live in southern California think the weather there is always the same.

10.____ The weather in southern California is always the same.

11.____ During periods of the hot, dry Santa Ana wind, firefighters in California expect more fires.

12.____ Usually, a Santa Ana wind only lasts three or four days. The longest Santa Ana period was in 1957, and it lasted a month.

Talking and Writing

With your classmates, use these questions as starting points for a discussion of ideas presented in the essay. Then select a question and write a short paper on the topic.

1. How does the author describe the behavior of her neighbors so that you know she had good reason to be afraid during a Santa Ana wind? Does she need to directly tell the reader that she was afraid?

How does the author illustrate her belief that the Santa Ana wind affects how people in Los Angeles feel and act? Give specific examples. How does the author make the reader feel the tension?

2. How do the author's descriptions of other people's experiences add to the essay? How do the reports from other people in Los Angeles, Switzerland, and Israel compare with her own impressions?

3. Have you had an experience with a violent force of nature, such as a snowstorm, a tornado, an earthquake, or a hurricane? (Or do you know someone who has had this kind of experience?) Write a short paper summarizing what happened, or describe the experience to the class.

4. Do you think the weather of a region influences the character of the people in the area? (What does the author mean by the last two sentences of the essay?) Or do you think people aren't affected by the weather?

For example, if you lived in New England, how do you think long, cold, snowy winters might affect your point of view? If you live in southern California, what do you think of this essay's point?

5. Write a short paper about the weather where you live. Describe what you like and don't like about it.

   If you've moved from one part of the world to another, or from one part of your country to a new home, how do the climates differ?

More Ideas

1. Libraries and bookstores will have information about forces of nature such as blizzards, typhoons, monsoons, earthquakes, volcanos, and tornados. You could give a short talk to the class or write a short paper on one of these topics.

   For example, you could find out about earthquakes. What makes them happen? Where do they occur? How do they affect people's lives? You could describe a recent earthquake, or you could describe an earthquake that happened in the past, such as the severe 1906 earthquake in San Francisco, California.

   If you have personal experience with earthquakes, tornados, or hurricanes, or you know someone who does, you could include those first-hand impressions in your report. (Bring books with photographs to class, if you can.)

2. Find out more about Los Angeles and give a talk to the class, or write a short paper.

   For example, Los Angeles is a relatively new city, with low buildings spread out over many miles. How many people live in Los Angeles and its suburbs? What do different parts of the city and southern California look like?

   Find out about the history of Los Angeles. For example, what were the Spanish missions?

   You could also describe Hollywood, the La Brea tar pits, or places near Los Angeles such as Death Valley, Disneyland, or Las Vegas, Nevada.

3. Find out about northern California. (The city of San Francisco is on a peninsula and the weather there is often cool and foggy.) For example, you could describe Yosemite, Alcatraz, or the Golden Gate Bridge.

Building Vocabulary

Complete the following sentences, using the appropriate words from the list. Be sure to use the correct form of each word.

easily	easy	ease	uneasy

1. a) A Santa Ana wind is coming. There is something _____ in the Los Angeles air this afternoon.

   b) This test isn't very hard; it's really _____.

   c) I know this information. I can write this exam _____.

   d) You've got to park that car in a very small space. You'd better _____ it in slowly.

is due	cut my losses	sirens	flammable
surf	trespassing	whining	inflammable

2. a) She's expecting a baby. The baby _____ on Friday.

   b) When I was in the supermarket, I heard a mother say to her child, "Stop _____ ."

   c) We were playing poker, and I was losing. I decided to quit while I was ahead. I _____ and left the game.

   d) On the first day of every month, the rent _____ .

   e) If you see a sign that says, " _____ material," don't light a match.

   f) Walking on somebody's private property is called _____.

g) A few minutes after I called the police, I heard the _____

h) If you see a sign that says " _____ material," don't light a match.

i) A _____ board is a piece of wood you stand on to ride the ocean waves to the shore.

unmanageable	clot	invariably
cast	folk	depressed

3. a) Because the Santa Ana is hot and dry, its presence _____ means fire.

b) Before a Santa Ana wind, the sky had a yellow _____.

c) My friend broke his leg and the doctors put it in a _____.

d) Traditional wisdom that might not have a scientific basis is called _____ wisdom.

e) A traditional dance is called a _____ dance.

f) If something's very hard to control, we say it's _____.

g) Someone who has problems and isn't happy might say, "I'm _____."

h) If you cut yourself and your blood doesn't _____, you've got a problem. The cut won't stop bleeding.

Two Faces of Eventide

Ivor Shapiro

Before You Begin . . .

Old age is sometimes described as a chance to finally do everything you always wanted to do, a kind of second childhood. It's also said to be a miserable time, when you're lonely, sick, and poor. In the following essay, the author explores these two images of old age.

Ivor Shapiro, a journalist in Toronto, wrote this essay in 1989 for the Canadian magazine *Saturday Night*.

You'll want to read this essay twice, the first time to get a general idea of what the author wants to say about the lives of the elderly in Canada. The second time you read the essay, you'll pick up more vocabulary and better understand how the author makes his points.

For a summary of the author's ideas, see the exercises in the section "Understanding the Essay," after the essay.

To practice using some of the vocabulary, take a look at the section "Building Vocabulary," at the end of the chapter.

Before you read this essay, your class could talk about how people in your society think of old age. What role do the elderly people you know play in the community and in the family?

And before you read this essay, here are a few terms to know:

- age-discrimination: something that denies people their rights simply because they are older
- age-specific: directly related to someone's age, such as a government payment
- ageism: discrimination against older people. We also use the term *racism* to mean "discrimination against people because of their race," and *sexism* to mean "discrimination based on gender."
- elderly: old people, sometimes called senior citizens
- pension: small income provided by the government to the elderly; also, some jobs give pensions
- retirement: age when people stop working, such as 65

Two Faces of Eventide

Ivor Shapiro

The meaning of the word "old" is under renovation.[1] It used to be that young people were meant to feel sorry for old people, to offer them a seat on the bus and a kind word, loudly spoken. Now old age has been declared *fun*. Today's pensioner[2] is expected to be busy with hobbies and volunteer work when not attending "elderobics"[3] classes or touring the world. *Discovery* magazine, a lifestyle magazine for the fifty-plus market,[4] offers features on holiday ideas, tax reform, and work opportunities for retirees[5] along with columns on living with wrinkles and the art of grandparenting. It all adds up to what Norman Blackie, executive director of the Winnipeg-based Canadian Association on Gerontology,[6] calls a growing national awareness that getting old 10 does not mean getting ill and decrepit,[7] that ageing is "not a negative situation but a continuation of a very natural process."

Yet the front seats on the bus are still reserved for "the elderly and handicapped," and when someone hits sixty-five[8] she or he becomes automatically entitled to tax breaks[9] and old-age security payments. It seems that we cannot make up our mind about old people: are they frail[10] and needy, as we used to think, or are they the Brave New Old, healthy enough, wealthy enough, and wise enough[11] to fly south for the winter?[12] The two portraits manage to survive because, obviously, there are enough people around to act as live models for both. But the real problem is that two stereotypes are not better than one. 20

There was widespread praise last summer for a report of the Commons Committee on Human Rights[13] that recommended concerted government action to eliminate ageism and age-discrimination. But the all-party[14] report unwittingly highlighted[15] the contemporary confusion about the meaning of "old." In a grand

---

1 **under renovation:** being changed and improved
2 **pensioner:** person who receives a pension
3 **"elderobics":** exercise activities for old people
4 **fifty-plus market:** the group of people over fifty years old who might buy a specific product
5 **retirees:** retired people
6 **Winnipeg-based Canadian Association on Gerontology:** organization that studies old age, with its offices in Winnipeg, Manitoba
7 **decrepit:** weak and worn-out (generally used to describe an old building)
8 **hits sixty-five:** (slang) becomes sixty-five years of age
9 **tax break:** lower taxes
10 **frail:** weak; easily broken
11 **healthy enough, wealthy enough, and**

wise enough: from an old saying: "Early to bed and early to rise makes a man healthy, wealthy, and wise."
12 **fly south for the winter:** Some birds in North America fly south for the winter, returning in the spring to their northern homes. Some retired people have enough money to spend winters in the southern United States, where the weather's warm.
13 **Commons Committee on Human Rights:** group from the federal government that studies people's rights in society
14 **all-party:** all three Canadian political parties (Tories, Liberals, and the New Democratic Party)
15 **unwittingly highlighted:** accidentally called attention to

blitz of good intentions, the report covered everything from the injustice of mandatory[16] retirement to the shortage of nursing-home[17] beds. The committee members were trying to respond to the diverse concerns[18] of a vast body of Canadians who have nothing in common but the fact that they are no longer thought of as young. In the process, the M.P.s[19] lumped[20] everyone over sixty-five together under the heading of "elderly," which makes about as much sense as would a report on Canada's "youth" that dealt with the needs both of teenagers and of adults in their late-twenties. And in one startling[21] recommendation, the report even managed to paint both contrasting pictures of ageing in a single sentence, urging the federal and provincial governments[22] to move towards the complete abolition[23] of mandatory retirement, "with the sole exception of a limited class of occupations directly involving the public safety." Which is it to be, then? Is age irrelevant[24] to ability, or are people above retirement age automatically prone to sickness and incapacity—and therefore poor candidates for employment whether or not the public safety is involved?

40 Toronto gerontologist Blossom Wigdor's answer is unequivocal.[25] The age of sixty-five, she says, is an age remarkable[26] only for its unremarkability. While the same could be said, strictly speaking, of any age, there are some numbers that can serve as convenient, if approximate, markers.[27] Somewhere between eighteen and twenty-one, adolescence is over and young adulthood begins. And most people older than seventy-five or eighty can expect to discover what frailty and chronic illness are about. But contrary to popular belief,[28] little distinguishes the physical and mental state of the average fifty-year-old from that of a person twenty years older.

That means, of course, that there is no justice at all in requiring someone to **50** retire at the age of sixty-five (except perhaps from the biased point of view of an unemployed twenty-five-year-old for whom a job gets created in the process). Certainly society would be well rid of a traditional attitude to ageing that has largely involved writing off[29] the old as pathetic and useless. But it would be a

16 mandatory: forced
17 nursing home: special home for group of elderly in poor health
18 diverse concerns: different interests
19 M.P.s: members of Parliament, the people in the Canadian government who make the laws
20 lumped together: put together in a single group
21 startling: surprising
22 the federal and provincial government: The federal government is the government for all of Canada, with the capital located in Ottawa, Ontario.
Each province of Canada has its own government. For example, the capital of the province of Ontario is Toronto, and the capital of Nova Scotia is Halifax.
In the United States, the federal government is located in Washington, D.C., and each state has its own government. For example, the capital of Illinois is Springfield, and the capital of California is Sacramento.
23 abolition: official and legal end of a custom
24 irrelevant: has nothing to do with
25 unequivocal: clear; without a doubt
26 remarkable: unusual
27 marker: something that's used to indicate a beginning or an end
28 contrary to popular belief: everyone assumes this is true but it isn't
29 writing off: ignoring; dismissing

pity if that foolishness were replaced by an idealized vision[30] that is no less unresponsive to reality.

The dawning mythology of the Brave New Old, active and happy in the sunset of their lives, ignores the physical losses that frequently come with advancing years. Hearing and eyesight tend to deteriorate, bones become brittle, the risk from infection grows. It's sad, it's scary, but it's true. And each passing year brings closer the certainty of death. At seventy-two, Fred Atkinson is less sanguine[31] than resigned[32] about his advancing years. "If there were something I could do about it I surely would," says the retired tool-and-die maker. "It's hard to express the feeling that you have. It's not frustration or anything like that, it's, oh, I don't know, the feeling that you've lived your life and now you're in the decline."[33]

When Atkinson had to retire after forty-three years at Moncton's now-closed railway yards, life lost some of its meaning. Much of the rest went when his wife died two years ago. "I think the happiest time of my life was when the children were small and my wife gave them a bath and put them to bed. At least you knew where they were." Later came the worries of parenting three adolescents, and then the pain of watching his household shrink.[34] "Now it's just me and the cat." And the placid collie shepherd dog that he babysits for his daughter during the day while she is at work. For Atkinson, being old means relying on other people to blow the snow and mow the lawn[35] (well, he never did enjoy blowing snow or mowing lawns), and it also means a diminished sexual self-image.[36] ("You see a nice-looking woman and you kind of look at her, and then you go by a plate-glass window and you look at yourself and say, 'Who's that old guy?'") But above all, ageing means loneliness. Atkinson can drive his car to a shopping mall and run into someone he knows and have a coffee, or he can go out to visit. But seeking company requires effort, especially in winter, and he finds himself spending a lot of time at home alone. "When you're used to working with two or three thousand people, and you're reduced to talking to yourself or the dog or the cat, it's quite a change."

Of course, just as lots of people manage to short-circuit[37] frailty, dying quickly and easily after long, healthy lives, many find ways to avoid loneliness too. In every society, old age is lived out in ways too diverse to fit either the former myth[38] of the rocking knitter or the current myth of the Amazon explorer, and the differences are dictated[39] not just by medical condition but by personality,

60

70

80

---

30 idealized vision: point of view that is not realistic
31 sanguine: optimistic
32 resigned: (here) accepts something he can't avoid
33 in the decline: going down
34 shrink: get smaller
35 mow the lawn: cut the grass around the house

36 self-image: how someone thinks of himself or herself
37 short-circuit: (here) stop something from happening
38 myth: story that a society uses to illustrate its point of view
39 dictated: (here) determined or guided by

outlook, and circumstance. If Fred Atkinson incarnates[40] everyone's fears about
90 ageing, the sprightly Olga Chapman, who lives around the corner, is an icon[41] of
hope.

When her grandmother turned seventy, Chapman remembers, "We thought,
'She's getting old—we'd better buy mauve[42] clothes for her.'" Now eighty-two,
the widow Chapman has in the past ten years visited Spain, Bermuda, Morocco,
Hawaii, and the west coasts of Canada and the United States. In the past week the
diminutive[43] retired bookkeeper had been out to a meal with each of her sisters
and hosted a dinner party for eight.[44] Without being asked, she recites the menu
with glowing pride: "Spinach lasagne, spaghetti and meat sauce, french bread and
salad, and homemade apple pie." And she says: "I still don't think I'm old
100 enough to wear mauve."

But Olga Chapman is healthy enough and well-off[45] enough to take those
trips. For some women her age, retirement is less fun. There are two single
women over sixty-five for every single man in the same age group and many
widows,[46] having earned little or nothing in the way of pensionable income
themselves, also get no survivors' benefits from their dead husbands' obsolete[47]
pensions. The result is that about half of Canada's older single women have
incomes ranging between $700 and $1,100 a month, including all government
benefits. Without private means and family support, a woman depending on that
kind of income while living in a major city and paying rent can be living in
110 squalor and loneliness.

Today's employment patterns should gradually produce higher numbers of
women who draw pension benefits from contributory plans (including Canada
Pension Plan and Quebec Pension Plan). New diets and other salutary trends
should gradually raise men's life expectancies.[48] At the same time, the nation
continues to watch its hair turn grey at an accelerating[49] rate. Where five per cent
of Canada's population was over sixty-five at the turn of this century, thirteen per
cent will have passed that age in 2001—and eighteen per cent in 2021, when the
health-watching, affluent[50] baby boomers[51] are drawing their pensions.

Should we be worried about those numbers? There have been dire predictions

---

40 incarnates: is a living representation of something
41 icon: image; representation
42 mauve: a moderate shade of the color purple
43 diminutive: very small
44 hosted a dinner party for eight: invited eight friends to dinner as her guests
45 well-off: financially comfortable
46 widow: woman whose husband has died
47 obsolete: not useful anymore
48 men's life expectancies: average number of years most men live
49 accelerating: rapidly increasing
50 affluent: wealthy
51 baby boomers: After World War II ended in 1945, there was a "baby boom" for about twenty years in North America. Many more babies were born during this period than had been born in previous or subsequent generations. As the baby boomers approach middle age, we refer to the "greying of America."

of a bankrupt pension system,[52] and of a health-care crisis that can be avoided [120]
only by diverting money from hospitals to home care and self-help assistance for
the chronically ill.[53] Both scenarios are vigorously debated among the experts,
with some advocates[54] for today's elderly standing on the sidelines[55] urging
everyone to stop talking about ageing as a problem. It's not a problem, they say,
it's simply a period in people's lives that presents, like any other period, its own
special joys and challenges. But many of those same advocates unwittingly
entrench stereotypes by grouping vastly different concerns under the heading of
"seniors' issues."

Gerontologists identify two distinct groups, the young-old and the old-old,
differentiated by each individual's physical, emotional, and socio-economic well- [130]
being. The labels serve a limited purpose, as sociological shorthand,[56] but they
have nothing to do with chronology.[57] Independent Olga Chapman is theoretically
well into the years of frailty,[58] but she remains young-old, while the younger Fred
Atkinson who still enjoys good health shows signs of fast becoming old-old
emotionally.

The radically varied needs and lifestyles of older Canadians raise questions
about age-specific government payments, tax benefits, transportation
concessions, and miscellaneous private-sector discounts. Shouldn't those breaks
go to people who really need them, whatever their age, rather than to all people
born before an arbitrarily[59] selected year? A single mother on welfare might be [140]
pretty grateful to be eligible[60] for discounted goods and services that are now
enjoyed by all people above sixty-five, whatever their circumstances.

It is not just in this country that age-specific government programmes have
served to dilute compassion[61] with confusion. "A case can be made," writes U.S.
gerontologist Bernice Neugarten, "that at the same time that age itself is
becoming less relevant in the society, legislators and administrators have been
proliferating[62] laws and regulations that are age-based. In the legitimate concern
over the welfare of older people, we have seized upon age as the convenient
dimension for creating programs of income maintenance, housing, transportation,
health services, social services, and tax benefits." The effect, Neugarten says, in [150]
her collection of essays, *Age or Need? Public Policies for Older People*, is to
reinforce "the misperception of 'the old' as a problem group."

---

52 dire predictions of a bankrupt pension system: Some people have said the Canadian pension system will run out of money in the future. (In the United States, the social security system is said to be in a similar situation.)
53 chronically ill: constantly ill
54 advocates: people who support a cause or an idea
55 standing on the sidelines: watching the activity but not participating

56 shorthand: (here) quick way to describe something
57 chronology: numerical order of dates
58 well into the years of frailty: past the beginning of the weak and fragile years
59 arbitrarily: done for no particular reason
60 eligible: qualified to receive something
61 compassion: sympathy and a desire to help
62 proliferating: producing more and more

But in Canada at least, substantial policy changes are politically unpalatable[63] right now. After the drubbing[64] received by the Tories over their 1985 attempt to partially de-index pensions,[65] the people on Parliament Hill[66] are in no hurry to take on[67] the seniors' lobby[68] by touching the universality of benefits. Yet benefits aside, it is hard to see why seniors' advocates and programmes routinely try to respond to the diverse needs of *both* the old-old *and* the young-old. By not choosing one or the other, they do nothing to sharpen the blurry public vision of a
160   subject with which no one is entirely comfortable.

It is simply not a matter of years. Healthy and relatively wealthy retirees are able to fight their own battles, between trips. But for people who cannot greet retirement as a fun time, for those whose daily war is fought against sickness or poverty or loneliness or all three, being a "senior citizen" doesn't help a damn, and the new face of ageing is just so much greasepaint.[69]

---

63 unpalatable: unpleasant-tasting
64 drubbing: beating
65 attempt to partially de-index pensions: if the pensions are "de-indexed," they won't go up when the cost of living goes up
66 people on Parliament Hill: lawmaking body of the federal government of Canada

67 take on: work against
68 lobby: organization of people trying to influence the members of the government to vote in specific ways
69 greasepaint: heavy makeup used by actors in the theater

Understanding the Essay

Work individually or with another student to answer these comprehension questions and review the author's points in this essay.

Mark each of the following sentences true or false. If the statement is true, explain further. If it's false, correct the sentence.

1.___ The meaning of the word *old* hasn't changed.

2.___ Young people have been expected to be jealous of old people.

3.___ According to the author, an elderly person today is expected to be busy with hobbies and volunteer work, or touring the world.

4.___ The front seats on the bus are reserved only for the handicapped.

5.___ Gerontology means a study of heart problems.

6.___ When someone turns sixty-five, he or she has to pay more in taxes.

7.___ According to the author, we have two stereotypes of old age: 1) the elderly are frail and needy, and 2) the elderly are rich and healthy.

8.___ Mandatory retirement means a worker can retire whenever he or she wants.

9.___ Fred Atkinson thinks old age is a lot of fun.

10.___ Olga Chapman thinks old age is a lonely period.

11.___ There are more single elderly men than single elderly women in North America today.

12.___ Many widows are poor.

13.___ Fewer women will have their own pensions in the twenty-first century than do today.

14.___ There will be more old people in the twenty-first century than there are today.

Talking and Writing

With your classmates, use these questions as starting points for a discussion of ideas presented in the essay. Then select a question and write a short paper on the topic.

1. Why does the author think two stereotypes of old age aren't better than one stereotype? Do you agree? Or do you think people over 65 have more in common than the author of this essay suggests?

2. How does the author use his descriptions of Fred Atkinson and Olga Chapman to illustrate his points?

   How do income and health affect an older person's lifestyle? How would someone's activities before retirement affect his or her life after retirement?

   Think of different people you know who are aged 65 or over. How do their points of view differ? How do their lifestyles compare with the stereotypes described in this essay? (In what ways are they like Fred Atkinson and Olga Chapman, as the author describes them in the essay?)

3. At the beginning of the essay, the author describes young people on the bus offering seats to old people. Why do you think the author begins his discussion of the elderly in society with this example?

4. It would be interesting to ask people about the role of the elderly in society, and share the answers with the class. You could ask two questions:

   a) In general, what do you think of how the elderly are treated in this society?

   b) Specifically, do the elderly people you know live in their own homes, in nursing homes, or with their children? What are their lives like? How would you describe the relationships between the people you know and their older or younger relatives?

5. In North America, it's generally the responsibility of the women in a family to take care of the needs of elderly relatives living at home, or to visit older relatives if they live elsewhere. Is this true in other societies, as well? Would you change this custom? Why or why not?

6. What do you think it would be like for an old person to live with younger relatives, from the point of view of either the old person or the younger family?

   Is it always the same experience, for all old people and all younger families? What factors would influence this situation?

7. Write a short paper, or write a letter to the newspaper editor or your local government representative, describing what society should do for the elderly who want to stay in their own homes, or in the homes of their families.

   For example, sometimes a family wants an elderly relative to live with them, but the relative is in poor health and needs to be taken care of during the day.

   How would you solve this problem? What are the needs of the elderly person and the younger family in this situation? Do you think the government should help?

More Ideas

1. What would you like to be doing when you're over sixty-five? If you're over sixty-five now, is old age what you expected?

   How is your point of view on old age affected by how old you are now? How do you think younger and older people see the aging process?

2. You could ask one or two people how they feel about retirement and then report back to the class, or write a short paper describing their points of view.

   Ask a young person: When would you like to retire? What would you like to do then? (Do you have any projects you don't have time for now, or projects you'd like to continue?) What do you think will be good and bad about retirement?

   Ask a retired person: How does retirement compare with what you expected? What's good and bad about retirement? What should society do for retired people? How do other retired people live?

3. Should all elderly people receive discounts on transportation, housing, and medical care? If you were a retired person, what might your point of view be? If you were a working person, what might your point of view be? Why?

   How do you think the government should handle this situation? (How can we avoid having different parts of society fighting over "slices of the pie?")

4. Who should provide financial support for the elderly? Families? Government? (If you were a retired person, where would you prefer to get your financial support?)

   If the government provides all the financial support for retirees, where should it get the money? From special taxes? From the paychecks of working people, before they retire? (What if someone is unemployed, or is at home taking care of children?)

5. Do you think people with positions in public safety, such as bus drivers or presidents of countries, should retire at sixty-five? Do you think all people should be forced to stop driving automobiles after age sixty-five?

6. To find out about organizations of the elderly in your area, check your phone book, or check with your local government or library.

You could give a brief talk to the class (or write a short paper) about a special service that's offered to the elderly, such as legal help, medical care, or help with housing, as well as social activities. Or you could describe a service that some elderly need but don't have.

7. Libraries and bookstores have books by the elderly describing old age from medical, social, and financial points of view.

Suggested reading: *Tell Me a Riddle* by Tillie Olsen; *Songs of Experience: An Anthology of Literature on Growing Old*, edited by Margaret Fowler and Priscilla McCutcheon; *The View from 80* by Malcolm Crowley; *In the Fullness of Time* by Avis D. Carlson; *Growing Old in America*, edited by Beth B. Hess and Elizabeth W. Markson.

Building Vocabulary

1. Complete the following sentences, using the appropriate words from this list. Be sure to use the correct form of each word.

chronologically	chronic	host or hostess
age-specific	nursing home	guest

a) These dates are arranged in _____ order: 1912, 1935, 1968, 1991.

b) When you have a party at your house, you're the _____. If you attend a party at someone else's house, you're the _____.

c) Laws that are based on a person's age are said to be _____.

d) A person who has a long-term illness is _____ ill.

e) Most elderly in North America aren't living in _____.

2. Use these words to fill in the blanks in the following sentences. Be sure to change the form of the word if necessary.

break	well off	change my mind
mandatory	made up my mind	resign

a) If you're over sixty-five in North America, you get a tax _____ every year.

b) I can't decide which one to buy. I just can't _____.

c) At 1:00, we stop working and take a lunch _____.

d) I was going to vote for that candidate but I've _____.

e) Fred Atkinson was _____ to old age, but he didn't like it.

f) If your company requires you to retire at a certain age, your firm has _____ retirement.

g) If you're financially comfortable, we say you're _____.

h) She _____ from her job. Her last day was Tuesday.

Snapshot of a Dog

James Thurber

Before You Begin . . .

A snapshot is a quick, informal photograph. In this story, the author describes life with his family's dog, Rex, as Thurber and his brothers were growing up in the American Midwest, in Columbus, Ohio.

The humorous writing of James Thurber (1894–1961), often accompanied by his unique drawings, originally appeared in *The New Yorker* magazine and has been well known and loved by generations of readers. In addition to his stories about growing up in Ohio, James Thurber wrote about his adult life in New York and France, where he was a reporter.

You may want to read the beginning of the story together in class. How does the author show how he feels about Rex?

For a summary of the story's events, see the section "Understanding the Story."

To practice using some of the vocabulary in this story, take a look at the section "Building Vocabulary" at the end of the chapter.

Snapshot of a Dog

James Thurber

I ran across a dim photograph of him the other day, going through some old things. He's been dead twenty-five years. His name was Rex[1] (my two brothers and I named him when we were in our early teens) and he was a bull terrier.[2] "An American bull terrier," we used to say, proudly; none of your English bulls. He had one brindle eye[3] that sometimes made him look like a clown and sometimes reminded you of a politician with derby hat[4] and cigar. The rest of him was white except for a brindle saddle that always seemed to be slipping off and a brindle stocking on a hind leg. Nevertheless, there was a nobility[5] about him. He was big and muscular and beautifully made. He never lost his dignity even when trying to accomplish the extravagant[6] tasks[7] my brothers and myself used to set for him. One of these was the bringing of a ten-foot wooden rail into the yard[8] through the back gate. We would throw it out into the alley and tell him to go get it. Rex was as powerful as a wrestler, and there were not many things that he couldn't manage somehow to get hold of with his great jaws[9] and lift or drag to wherever he wanted to put them, or wherever we wanted them put. He could catch the rail at the balance[10] and lift it clear of the ground and trot[11] with great confidence toward the gate. Of course, since the gate was only four feet wide or so, he couldn't bring the rail in broadside. He found that out when he got a few terrific jolts,[12] but he wouldn't give up. He finally figured out how to do it, by dragging the rail, holding onto one end, growling.[13] He got a great, wagging[14] satisfaction out of his work. We used to bet kids who had never seen Rex in action that he could catch a baseball thrown as high as they could throw it. He almost never let us down.[15] Rex could hold a baseball with ease in his mouth, in one cheek, as if it were a chew of tobacco.

He was a tremendous fighter, but he never started fights. I don't believe he liked to get into them, despite the fact that he came from a line of fighters. He never went for another dog's throat but for one of its ears (that teaches a dog a

1 Rex: king (Latin)
2 bull terrier: type of dog; bull terriers are short and strong
3 brindle eye: the dog's fur was gray with darker spots around his eye
4 derby hat: old-fashioned kind of hat
5 nobility: (here) high morals and honesty
6 extravagant: (here) large and complicated
7 tasks: assignments or jobs
8 yard: (here) area of land surrounding a house
9 great jaws: large, strong bones and muscles

in his mouth
10 catch the rail at the balance: catch the middle of the rail and keep the rail from touching the ground
11 trot: walk very quickly
12 jolts: sharp blows
13 growling: the low, threatening sound a dog makes
14 wagging: happy motion a dog makes with its tail
15 let us down: disappointed us

lesson), and he would get his grip, close his eyes, and hold on.[16] He could hold on for hours. His longest fight lasted from dusk[17] until almost pitch-dark, one
30 Sunday. It was fought in East Main Street in Columbus with a large, snarly nondescript[18] that belonged to a big colored man. When Rex finally got his ear grip, the brief whirlwind of snarling[19] turned to screeching. It was frightening to listen to and to watch. The Negro boldly picked the dogs up somehow and began swinging them around his head, and finally let them fly like a hammer in a hammer throw, but although they landed ten feet away with a great plump, Rex still held on.

The two dogs eventually worked their way to the middle of the car tracks,[20] and after a while two or three streetcars were held up by the fight. A motorman tried to pry Rex's jaws open with a switch rod; somebody lighted a fire and made
40 a torch of a stick and held that to Rex's tail, but he paid no attention. In the end, all the residents and storekeepers in the neighborhood were on hand, shouting this, suggesting that. Rex's joy of battle, when battle was joined, was almost tranquil.[21] He had a kind of pleasant expression during fights, not a vicious[22] one, his eyes closed in what would have seemed to be sleep had it not been for the turmoil of the struggle.[23] The Oak Street Fire Department finally had to be sent for—I don't know why nobody thought of it sooner. Five or six pieces of apparatus[24] arrived, followed by a battalion chief. A hose was attached and a powerful stream of water was turned on the dogs. Rex held on for several moments more while the torrent buffeted him[25] about like a log in a freshet. He
50 was a hundred yards away from where the fight started when he finally let go.

The story of that Homeric[26] fight got all around town, and some of our relatives looked upon the incident as a blot[27] on the family name. They insisted that we get rid of[28] Rex, but we were very happy with him, and nobody could have made us give him up. We would have left town with him first, along any road there was to go. It would have been different, perhaps, if he'd ever started fights, or looked for trouble. But he had a gentle disposition. He never bit a person in the ten strenuous years that he lived, nor ever growled at anyone except prowlers.[29] He killed cats, that is true, but quickly and neatly and without especial malice,[30] the way men kill certain animals. It was the only thing he did that we
60 could never cure him of doing. He never killed, or even chased, a squirrel. I don't

16 **hold on:** not let go
17 **dusk:** beginning of night
18 **nondescript:** dog of no particular type
19 **snarling:** growling and showing teeth
20 **to the middle of the car tracks:** Some cities, including Toronto and San Francisco, have a local train that runs down the middle of the street on its own tracks, separated from the traffic of cars and buses. This train is also called a *streetcar* or a *trolley.*
21 **tranquil:** calm; serene
22 **vicious:** mean and cruel

23 **struggle:** fight
24 **apparatus:** (here) fire engine
25 **torrent buffeted him:** powerful stream of water tossed him
26 **Homeric:** like a hero (Homer was a poet in ancient Greece.)
27 **blot:** (here) bad mark
28 **get rid of:** give away or throw out
29 **prowlers:** strangers on private property, looking for things to steal
30 **malice:** desire to harm others

know why. He had his own philosophy about such things. He never ran barking[31] after wagons or automobiles. He didn't seem to see the idea in pursuing[32] something you couldn't catch, or something you couldn't do anything with, even if you did catch it. A wagon was one of the things he couldn't tug along with his mighty jaws, and he knew it. Wagons, therefore, were not part of his world.

Swimming was his favorite recreation. The first time he ever saw a body of water (Alum Creek), he trotted nervously along the steep bank for a while, fell to barking[33] wildly, and finally plunged in from a height of eight feet or more. I shall always remember that shining, virgin dive. Then he swam upstream and back just for the pleasure of it, like a man. It was fun to see him battle upstream against a stiff current,[34] struggling and growling every foot of the way. He had as much fun in the water as any person I have known. You didn't have to throw a stick in the water to get him to go in. Of course, he would bring back a stick to you if you did throw one in. He would even have brought back a piano if you had thrown one in.

That reminds me of the night, way after midnight, when he went a-roving in the light of the moon[35] and brought back a small chest of drawers[36] that he found somewhere—how far from the house nobody ever knew; since it was Rex, it could easily have been half a mile. There were no drawers in the chest when he got it home, and it wasn't a good one—he hadn't taken it out of anybody's house; it was just an old cheap piece that somebody had abandoned on a trash[37] heap. Still, it was something he wanted, probably because it presented a nice problem in transportation. It tested his mettle.[38] We first knew about his achievement when, deep in the night, we heard him trying to get the chest up onto the porch. It sounded as if two or three people were trying to tear the house down.[39] We came downstairs and turned on the porch light. Rex was on the top step trying to pull the thing up, but it had caught somehow and he was just holding his own.[40] I suppose he would have held his own till dawn if we hadn't helped him. The next day we carted the chest miles away and threw it out. If we had thrown it out in a nearby alley, he would have brought it home again, as a small token of his integrity[41] in such matters. After all, he had been taught to carry heavy wooden objects about, and he was proud of his prowess.[42]

I am glad Rex never saw a trained police dog jump. He was just an amateur[43] jumper himself, but the most daring and tenacious[44] I have ever seen. He would take on any fence we pointed out to him. Six feet was easy for him, and he could

70

80

90

---

31 barking: making the sharp sound a dog makes
32 pursuing: following; chasing
33 fell to barking: began barking
34 current: steady movement of the water in one direction
35 a-roving in the light of the moon: old expression that describes nighttime adventures that might be illegal
36 chest of drawers: kind of wooden furniture for clothing
37 trash: garbage
38 tested his mettle: tested his courage
39 tear the house down: destroy the house
40 holding his own: keeping his position in the fight
41 integrity: honor
42 prowess: superior skill or strength
43 amateur: not professional
44 tenacious: keeps trying

do eight by making a tremendous leap and hauling himself over finally by his paws, grunting and straining; but he lived and died without knowing that twelve- and sixteen-foot walls were too much for him. Frequently, after letting him try to go over one for a while, we would have to carry him home. He would never have given up trying.

100   There was in his world no such thing as the impossible. Even death couldn't beat him down. He died, it is true, but only, as one of his admirers said, after "straight-arming[45] the death angel" for more than an hour. Late one afternoon he wandered home, too slowly and too uncertainly to be the Rex that had trotted briskly homeward up our avenue for ten years. I think we all knew when he came through the gate that he was dying. He had apparently taken a terrible beating, probably from the owner of some dog that he had got into a fight with. His head and body were scarred. His heavy collar[46] with the teeth marks of many a battle on it was awry; some of the big brass studs in it were sprung loose from the leather. He licked at our hands and, staggering,[47] fell, but got up again. We could

110 see that he was looking for someone. One of his three masters[48] was not home. He did not get home for an hour. During that hour the bull terrier fought against death as he had fought against the cold, strong current of Alum Creek, as he had fought to climb twelve-foot walls. When the person he was waiting for did come through the gate, whistling, ceasing to whistle,[49] Rex walked a few wabbly paces[50] toward him, touched his hand with his muzzle,[51] and fell down again. This time he didn't get up.

45 straight-arming: keeping away by holding the arm straight
46 collar: leather identity band around the neck
47 staggering: walking as though in pain or confused
48 masters: owners
49 ceasing to whistle: stopping whistling
50 wabbly paces: unsteady steps
51 muzzle: an animal's jaw and nose

Understanding the Story

1. Discuss in class the following incidents from the story, or write one or two paragraphs summarizing the answers to each question. You could also work in teams or small groups and then report back to the class.

    • Describe the time when Rex brought the ten-foot pole through the back gate. Where did Rex find the pole?

    • Summarize Rex's longest fight. What was Rex's mood? How did it finally end? (How did the narrator's relatives feel about this fight?)

    • How did Rex learn to swim? What did he do first?

    • Retell the story of the night when Rex dragged home the chest of drawers. Why did he do that?

2. What could Rex do with a baseball? How did the author and his brothers feel about this skill?

3. What was the one thing Rex couldn't be cured of doing? How does the narrator feel about this?

4. How high could Rex jump?

5. Why did Rex "straight-arm" the death angel for more than an hour at the end of the story?

Talking and Writing

With your classmates, use these questions as starting points for a discussion of ideas presented in the story. Then select a question and write an essay on the topic.

1. What does the last paragraph of the story tell us about Rex? What was Rex's attitude toward life?

    What kind of personality did Rex have? How is the author able to describe the personality of a dog that cannot speak? Why did the author use these particular examples to illustrate Rex's life?

    What do you think of Rex's personality? Do you like him? Why or why not?

2. What was the author's goal in writing this story? Was he successful? (Is this story believable?)

3. Why didn't the narrator want to give Rex up, even though his relatives wanted to get rid of the dog? Why were the narrator and his brothers happy with the dog? How do you think Rex influenced the narrator's life?

4. Do you think animals have personalities in the same way that people do?

5. Why would someone want to have a pet? Why would an animal want to live with a human?

6. What are the roles of animals in other societies?

7. Dogs have a reputation for loyalty ("man's best friend") and have traditionally been popular as pets in North America. Cats have a reputation for independence, and have recently become more popular, in part because North Americans have busier lifestyles than before. Would you rather have a dog or a cat as a pet? Why?

More Ideas

1. You can find collections of stories by James Thurber, such as *The Thurber Carnival*, in libraries and bookstores. One of his most famous stories, "The Secret Life of Walter Mitty," was made into a film starring Danny Kaye.

2. Libraries and bookstores will have information about animals. You could write a paper or give a short talk to the class describing the life of a wild animal, such as a wolf, a polar bear, a seal, or a whale. (Suggested reading: *Never Cry Wolf* by Farley Mowat; *White Fang* by Jack London; *Through a Window: My Thirty Years with Chimpanzees* by Jane Goodall.)

   A zoo will have information about different wild animals. (Here's an old joke: "I tried to call the zoo, but the lion was busy.")

   Check your phone book for the names of local animal rescue organizations that take care of animals without homes. They can provide magazines and brochures that describe how to care for animals.

3. If you have a pet, write a few paragraphs describing that animal's personality, giving examples of your pet's likes and dislikes.

   Or you could ask someone else to describe a pet's personality. Many adults share their lives with pets, or have happy memories of growing up with pets. You could also interview children about their experiences.

4. Do you think medical research should be performed on animals? How do we know if human lives will be saved?

   Should animals be used to test soaps and beauty supplies? Should animals be used in experiments to determine their ability to withstand pain, cold, or electrical shock?

Building Vocabulary

A phrasal verb is an expression that contains a verb and a preposition, such as *get up, give up,* or *bring back.*

Changing the prepositions in the phrasal verb can change the meaning completely. For example, *throw out* and *throw up* describe two different situations.

In this story, James Thurber uses a lot of phrasal verbs to describe his life with Rex. For example, in the first line of the story, the narrator says that he *ran across* a photograph of Rex. The phrase *run across* means "find something accidentally, without intentionally looking for it."

If we keep the same verb *to run* but change the preposition *across* to *away,* we have a different expression with a different meaning. The phrase *run away* means "escape."

Look at the sentences below and match each one to one of these word combinations: *run for, run out, run against.* Be sure to use the right verb tense. (Check your dictionary to confirm the definitions.)

1. John Kennedy _____ president in 1960 and won.

2. When John Kennedy ran for president, he _____ Richard Nixon.

3. We've got plenty of cheese but we've _____ of bread.

Sometimes the same expression can have more than one meaning. For example, what does *ran into* mean in each of the following sentences:

1. I was walking down the street last night and I *ran into* an old friend.
2. I wasn't looking where I was going and I *ran into* a wall.

Here's an old joke: "I knew a magician who was walking down the street and *turned into* an alley."

Now try combining the same verb (*to run*) with some of these prepositions: of, at, in, to, into, on, onto, up, upon, out, for, by, over, under, back, off, along, with, through, after, away, from, about, against.

How many examples can you find of expressions you've heard or used? Your class could also write sentences using some of the combinations you find.

Note that an expression might mean something different to you than it does to someone else. Use your dictionary to confirm some of the meanings. Some expressions might be slang or from a specific region of North America.

Match each of the following word combinations to the appropriate sentence. Be sure to use the correct tense for the verb. Check your dictionary to be sure of the definition. (How many other prepositions can you combine with the verb *to hold*?)

    a) hold up
    b) hold on
    c) hold over

1. After Rex got his grip on a dog's ear, he would sometimes close his eyes and _____ for hours.

2. During one fight between Rex and another dog, two or three streetcars were _____ by the struggle.

3. This movie is so popular that it was _____ another week.

A Conversation with My Father

Grace Paley

Before You Begin . . .

There's another story within this story. The narrator's father is old and sick, and he asks his daughter to tell a story. She creates a story that's based on the life of someone who lives across the street, but it's not the kind of story her father wanted.

So the narrator revises and expands the story into something she's happy with. Meanwhile, we learn a lot about how the narrator and her father see life differently.

Grace Paley's writing manages to be both serious and comical. Paley was born in 1922 in New York City to Russian Jewish immigrants, and at home her parents spoke only Russian and Yiddish. Her work reflects the Old-World point of view, as well as her own experiences in New York City. Paley is well known not only as a writer, but for her work in political causes.

This story is from Paley's collection *Enormous Changes at the Last Minute*.

Your class could read together the first page of this story and briefly discuss the points of view of the narrator and her father. How do they see life differently?

For a summary of the author's ideas, see the section "Understanding the Story."

To practice using some of the vocabulary in this story, take a look at the section "Building Vocabulary" at the end of the chapter.

A Conversation with My Father
Grace Paley

My father is eighty-six years old and in bed. His heart, that bloody motor,[1] is equally old and will not do certain jobs anymore. It still floods[2] his head with brainy light. But it won't let his legs carry the weight of his body around the house. Despite my metaphors,[3] this muscle failure[4] is not due to[5] his old heart, he says, but to a potassium shortage.[6] Sitting on one pillow, leaning on three, he offers last-minute[7] advice and makes a request.

"I would like you to write a simple story just once more," he says, "the kind de Maupassant[8] wrote, or Chekhov,[9] the kind you used to write. Just recognizable people and then write down what happened to them next."

I say, "Yes, why not? That's possible." I want to please him, though I don't   **10**
remember writing that way. I *would* like to try to tell such a story, if he means the kind that begins: "There was a woman . . ." followed by plot,[10] the absolute line between two points which I've always despised.[11] Not for literary reasons, but because it takes all hope away. Everyone, real or invented, deserves the open destiny[12] of life.

Finally I thought of a story that had been happening for a couple of years right across the street. I wrote it down, then read it aloud, "Pa," I said, "how about this? Do you mean something like this?"

Once in my time[13] there was a woman and she had a son. They lived nicely, in a small apartment in Manhattan.[14] This boy at about fifteen   **20**
became a junkie,[15] which is not unusual in our neighborhood. In order to maintain her close friendship with him, she became a junkie too. She said it was part of the youth culture, with which she felt very much at home.[16]

1 **motor:** machine
2 **flood:** overflowing of liquid (usually water)
3 **metaphor:** kind of expression that uses something to represent something else. For example: Old age is the sunset of life.
4 **failure:** opposite of success
5 **due to:** because of
6 **potassium shortage:** not enough potassium in the body for it to function well
7 **last-minute:** final moments before a deadline
8 **de Maupassant:** Guy de Maupassant was a nineteenth-century French writer
9 **Chekhov:** Anton Chekhov wrote short stories and dramas in late nineteenth-century Russia
10 **plot:** events in a story

11 **despised:** strongly disliked
12 **destiny:** future
13 **Once in my time:** a traditional story in English is introduced with "Once upon a time" to mean the story happened long ago. Here, the narrator has changed the story's beginning to show it's a current event and it's her story.
14 **Manhattan:** New York City is divided into five sections, called boroughs: Manhattan, Staten Island, Queens, Brooklyn, and the Bronx. When we think of New York City, we usually think of the busy downtown of Manhattan.
15 **junkie:** (slang) drug addict
16 **at home:** (here) comfortable and relaxed

123

After a while, for a number of reasons, the boy gave it all up and left the city and his mother in disgust.[17] Hopeless and alone, she grieved.[18] We all visit her.

"O.K., Pa, that's it," I said, "an unadorned and miserable tale."[19]

"But that's not what I mean," my father said. "You misunderstood me on purpose. You know there's a lot more to it. You know that. You left everything

30 out. Turgenev[20] wouldn't do that. Chekhov wouldn't do that. There are in fact Russian writers you never heard of, you don't have an inkling of,[21] as good as anyone, who can write a plain ordinary story, who would not leave out[22] what you have left out. I object not to facts but to people sitting in trees talking senselessly,[23] voices from who knows where . . ."

"Forget that one, Pa, what have I left out now? In this one?"

"Her looks,[24] for instance."

"Oh. Quite handsome, I think. Yes."

"Her hair?"

"Dark, with heavy braids, as though she were a girl or a foreigner."[25]

40 "What were her parents like, her stock? That she became such a person. It's interesting, you know."

"From out of town. Professional people. The first to be divorced in their county. How's that? Enough?" I asked.

"With you, it's all a joke," he said. "What about the boy's father? Why didn't you mention him? Who was he? Or was the boy born out of wedlock?"[26]

"Yes," I said. "He was born out of wedlock."

"For Godsakes, doesn't anyone in your stories get married? Doesn't anyone have the time to run down to City Hall[27] before they jump into bed?"

"No," I said. "In real life, yes. But in my stories, no."

50 "Why do you answer me like that?"

"Oh Pa, this is a simple story about a smart woman who came to N.Y.C.[28] full of interest love trust excitement very up to date,[29] and about her son, what a hard time she had in this world. Married or not, it's of small consequence."[30]

"It is of great consequence," he said.

---

17 in disgust: to have a feeling of irritation or dislike
18 grieved: felt pain because of a personal loss, such as when someone dies
19 unadorned and miserable tale: simple and very unhappy story
20 Turgenev: Ivan Turgenev was a Russian writer in the nineteenth century who described ordinary people and their lives
21 don't have an inkling of: don't have any idea of
22 leave out: not include
23 senselessly: without purpose or reason

24 her looks: her appearance
25 or a foreigner: here, the narrator is thinking of the braids of women immigrating to the United States in the early part of the twentieth century.
26 born out of wedlock: born to parents who are not married to each other
27 City Hall: the building for the city government and the place to register to get married
28 N.Y.C.: New York City
29 up to date: very recent
30 of small consequence: doesn't matter very much

"O.K.," I said.

"O.K. O.K. yourself," he said, "but listen. I believe you that she's good-looking, but I don't think she was so smart."

"That's true," I said. "Actually that's the trouble with stories. People start out fantastic. You think they're extraordinary, but it turns out as the work goes along, they're just average with a good education. Sometimes the other way around, the person's a kind of dumb innocent, but he outwits[31] you and you can't even think of an ending good enough."   **60**

"What do you do then?" he asked. He had been a doctor for a couple of decades[32] and then an artist for a couple of decades and he's still interested in details, craft, technique.[33]

"Well, you just have to let the story lie around till some agreement can be reached between you and the stubborn hero."

"Aren't you talking silly, now?" he asked. "Start again," he said. "It so happens I'm not going out this evening. Tell the story again. See what you can do this time."   **70**

"O.K.," I said. "But it's not a five-minute job." Second attempt:

Once, across the street from us, there was a fine handsome woman, our neighbor. She had a son whom she loved because she'd known him since birth (in helpless chubby infancy,[34] and in the wrestling, hugging ages, seven to ten, as well as earlier and later). This boy, when he fell into the fist of adolescence,[35] became a junkie. He was not a hopeless one. He was in fact hopeful, an ideologue and successful converter.[36] With his busy brilliance, he wrote persuasive articles for his high-school newspaper. Seeking a wider audience, using important connections, he drummed into Lower Manhattan newsstand distribution a periodical called *Oh! Golden*   **80**
Horse![37]

In order to keep him from feeling guilty (because guilt is the stony heart of nine tenths of all clinically diagnosed cancers[38] in America today, she said), and because she had always believed in giving bad habits room at home where one could keep an eye on them, she too became a junkie. Her kitchen was famous for a while—a center for intellectual addicts who knew what they were doing. A few felt artistic like Coleridge[39] and others

---

31 outwits: wins the competition by doing something very smart
32 decade: period of ten years
33 craft and technique: artist's skills
34 chubby infancy: when he was a fat baby
35 adolescence: teenage years
36 successful converter: (here) easily convinced people to change their ideas
37 horse: (slang) heroin, an addictive drug that is illegal in North America
38 clinically diagnosed cancers: a diagnosis is a patient's medical problem, as stated by the doctor. Here, the character of the mother in the story is inventing a connection between guilt and cancer to emphasize her point.
39 Coleridge: early nineteenth-century British author of the poem "The Ancient Mariner." Coleridge used the drug opium.

were scientific and revolutionary like Leary.[40] Although she was often high[41] herself, certain good mothering reflexes[42] remained, and she saw to it that there was lots of orange juice around and honey and milk and vitamin pills. However, she never cooked anything but chili, and that no more than once a week. She explained, when we talked to her, seriously, with neighborly concern, that it was her part in the youth culture and she would rather be with the young, it was an honor, than with her own generation.

One week, while nodding through an Antonioni film,[43] this boy was severely jabbed by the elbow of a stern[44] and proselytizing[45] girl, sitting beside him. She offered immediate apricots and nuts for his sugar level, spoke to him sharply, and took him home.

She had heard of him and his work and she herself published, edited, and wrote a competitive journal called *Man Does Live by Bread Alone*.[46] In the organic heat of her continuous presence he could not help but become interested once more in his muscles, his arteries, and nerve connections. In fact he began to love them, treasure them, praise them with funny little songs in *Man Does Live . . .*

the fingers of my flesh transcend[47]
my transcendental soul
the tightness in my shoulders end
my teeth have made me whole

To the mouth of his head (that glory of will and determination) he brought hard apples, nuts, wheat germ, and soybean oil. He said to his old friends, From now on, I guess I'll keep my wits about me. I'm going on the natch.[48] He said he was about to begin a spiritual deep-breathing journey. How about you too, Mom? he asked kindly.

His conversion was so radiant, splendid, that neighborhood kids his age began to say that he had never been a real addict at all, only a journalist[49] along for the smell of the story. The mother tried several times to give up

40 Leary: Timothy Leary was well known in the early 1960s for experimenting with mind-altering drugs such as LSD
41 high: (slang) to be high on a drug is like being drunk on alcohol
42 reflexes: automatic responses or instincts
43 nodding through an Antonioni film: the character's head keeps dropping because he's high on heroin
44 stern: severe; strict
45 proselytizing: attempting to convert other people to another religion

46 *Man Does Live by Bread Alone*: here, the character means man doesn't need meat to survive. The saying "man does not live by bread alone" comes from the Bible and means that people also need spiritual aspects to life.
47 transcend: to rise above, such as to be interested in spiritual topics rather than the material world
48 going on the natch: (slang) live naturally, without drugs
49 journalist: someone who writes for a newspaper

what had become without her son and his friends a lonely habit.[50] This
effort only brought it to supportable levels. The boy and his girl took their
electronic mimeograph[51] and moved to the bushy edge of another
borough. They were very strict. They said they would not see her again
until she had been off drugs for sixty days.

At home alone in the evening, weeping, the mother read and reread the
seven issues of *Oh! Golden Horse!* They seemed to her as truthful as ever.
We often crossed the street to visit and console.[52] But if we mentioned any
of our children who were at college or in the hospital or dropouts at
home,[53] she would cry out, "My baby! My baby!" and burst into terrible,
face-scarring, time-consuming tears. The End.

First my father was silent, then he said, "Number One: You have a nice sense
of humor. Number Two: I see you can't tell a plain story. So don't waste time."
Then he said sadly, "Number Three: I suppose that means she was alone, she was
left like that, his mother. Alone. Probably sick?"

I said, "Yes."

"Poor woman. Poor girl, to be born in a time of fools, to live among fools.
The end. The end. You were right to put that down. The end."

I didn't want to argue, but I had to say, "Well, it is not necessarily the end,
Pa."

"Yes," he said, "what a tragedy.[54] The end of a person."

"No, Pa," I begged him. "It doesn't have to be. She's only about forty. She
could be a hundred different things in this world as time goes on. A teacher or a
social worker. An ex-junkie! Sometimes it's better than having a master's in
education."[55]

"Jokes," he said. "As a writer that's your main trouble. You don't want to
recognize it. Tragedy! Plain tragedy! Historical tragedy! No hope. The end."

"Oh, Pa," I said. "She could change."

"In your own life, too, you have to look it in the face." He took a couple of
nitroglycerin.[56] "Turn to five," he said, pointing to the dial on the oxygen tank. He
inserted the tubes into his nostrils[57] and breathed deep. He closed his eyes and
said, "No."

I had promised the family to always let him have the last word[58] when
arguing, but in this case I had a different responsibility. That woman lives across
the street. She's my knowledge and my invention. I'm sorry for her. I'm not

50 habit: (here) drug addiction
51 electronic mimeograph: small printing press for producing newsletters
52 console: try to make someone feel better
53 dropouts at home: teenagers who left school before graduating and are still living at home
54 tragedy: story or drama that ends unhappily
55 master's in education: advanced university studies in the subject of teaching
56 nitroglycerin: drug used to treat heart problems
57 nostrils: two openings to the nose
58 let him have the last word: let him end the argument and think he won

going to leave her there in that house crying. (Actually neither would Life, which unlike me has no pity.)

Therefore: She did change. Of course her son never came home again. But right now, she's the receptionist in a storefront community clinic[59] in the East Village.[60] Most of the customers are young people, some old friends. The head doctor has said to her, "If we only had three people in this clinic with your experiences ..."

"The doctor said that?" My father took the oxygen tubes out of his nostrils and said, "Jokes. Jokes again."

"No, Pa, it could really happen that way, it's a funny world nowadays."

"No," he said. "Truth first. She will slide back.[61] A person must have character. She does not."

"No, Pa," I said. "That's it. She's got a job. Forget it. She's in that storefront working."

"How long will it be?" he asked. "Tragedy! You too. When will you look it in the face?"

---

59 storefront community clinic: medical center located in an empty store, usually helping people in the community who have no other health care
60 The East Village: part of Greenwich Village, a neighborhood in Manhattan that is a home for people with unusual lifestyles, including poets and artists
61 slide back: return to previous habits

Understanding the Story

Work individually or with another student to answer these comprehension questions and review the story's events.

Mark each of the following sentences true or false. If the statement is true, explain further. If it's false, correct the sentence.

1.____ The narrator's father is old but he's not sick.

2.____ The father's heart is like an old machine that will not do certain jobs anymore. His mind is fine but his legs don't work very well.

3.____ The father asks his daughter to paint him a picture.

4.____ The father wants a story that's complicated.

5.____ The daughter doesn't want to write a story in which there's no hope for the future.

6. Summarize the first version of the story the daughter wrote:

Once there was a _____ and she had a _____. They lived in a small apartment in _____, across the street.

When the boy was about fifteen, he became a _____. The mother became a junkie, too, in order to _____. She also said she felt _____ with the youth culture.

Later, the boy stopped being a junkie. He left the city and his mother. She felt _____ after her son left.

7. Summarize the second version of the story the daughter wrote:

Once there was a woman who lived across the street. When the son was an adolescent, he became a junkie. But he still wrote articles for his high-school _____. Then he started a newspaper called _____.

His mother became a junkie, too. Her kitchen was famous for a while because _____.

The son met a girl who was very interested in natural foods that are good for the body. She wrote a newspaper called _____. She took him home and convinced him to change his lifestyle.

The son gave up drugs so easily that other teenagers said _____. The mother tried to give up drugs but couldn't. Her neighbors tried to _____ her. But when people mentioned their own children, she would _____.

Talking and Writing

With your classmates, use these questions as starting points for a discussion of ideas presented in the story. Then select a question and write an essay on the topic.

1. Why wasn't the father happy with the story his daughter wrote? What did he want her to include in the story?

2. Why did the father and daughter disagree on the ending for the story?

   What did the father assume happens to the woman in the story? What does the daughter think happens at the end of the story, or could happen? Who do you agree with—the father or the daughter? Why?

3. What does the disagreement between the father and daughter tell us about how their philosophies are different? (What does the father mean by the last line in the story?)

   What other examples in the story show us that they have different points of view? How would you describe their relationship?

4. The daughter tells a story about a woman who has problems with drugs. Later, this woman overcomes her drug problems and gets a responsible job. Do you think people make major changes like this frequently? Why or why not? How does society respond when people "turn their lives around"?

5. Write a paragraph describing one of the characters in this story: the narrator; the father; the woman across the street; the son; the son's girlfriend.

More Ideas

1. Try writing a few paragraphs as a short story of your own. You could tell a true story about something that happened to you.

   Or you could invent a modern story, based on something or someone you know, the way the narrator of "A Conversation with My Father" wrote about the woman living across the street.

2. Try writing a traditional story you know, or creating a new one in the same style.

   A traditional story describes something that happened long ago and begins with "Once there was" or "Once upon a time" or "Long, long ago." Sometimes these stories are legends, used to explain the actions of human beings or the forces of nature. For example, the Iroquois Indians of North America have a legend that describes the world resting on the back of a giant turtle.

   If your class is made up of different nationalities, it would be interesting to see if different cultures have similar stories.

Building Vocabulary

Complete the following sentences, using the appropriate words from the list. Be sure to use the correct form of each word.

last-minute   plot   senseless

1. a) The series of events in a story is called a _____.

   b) Before I left this morning, they offered me some _____ advice.

   c) The father didn't like story characters talking _____.

tragedy   in disgust   adolescence   up to date

2. a) An _____ is someone in the years between childhood and adulthood.

   b) We listened to the radio to get the _____ news about the war.

    c) A story that ends in disappointment is called a _____ story.

    d) I really didn't like that movie, so I finally left _____.

console	turn out	habit
journalist	leave out	miserable

3. a) Someone who feels very unhappy is _____.

    b) I wasn't sure the mural I painted would be good, but it _____ fine.

    c) I couldn't include everything in the suitcase, so I _____ my swimsuit.

    d) He was very upset, so we _____ him.

    e) She wants to write for a newspaper, so she's studying _____.

    f) Many people think smoking cigarettes is a bad _____.

Forgiveness in Families

Alice Munro

Before You Begin . . .

Sometimes we use the word *outrageous* to describe an event so extreme we can hardly believe it happened. And when someone in the family's doing outrageous things, we're sure nobody else in the world could act like that.

In the following story, the narrator describes her brother, who has been doing unbelievable things since childhood. She feels a mixture of emotions: irritation, love, and frustration. Sometimes it's just funny to watch the way he lives.

Alice Munro was born in 1931 in a small town in southwest Ontario. Much of her writing is about growing up in the Scots-Irish community of her childhood. Later, as an adult, she lived in Vancouver, British Columbia, where she and her family had a bookstore. Munro now lives near where she grew up in Ontario.

One of the best known of Canadian writers, Alice Munro is most respected for her descriptions of complex and often contradictory human behavior. Most of her writing is in the form of the short story, but she's also written a novel, and some of her stories have been made into dramas for Canadian television. This story is from her collection, *Something I've Been Meaning to Tell You.*

You might want to read the first paragraph of this story together in class to get a sense of the story's informal style. It's written as though the narrator is talking to a close friend, or thinking to herself.

For a look at the language used in this story, see the section "Building Vocabulary" at the end of the chapter.

Forgiveness in Families

Alice Munro

I've often thought, suppose I had to go to a psychiatrist,[1] and he would want to know about my family background, naturally,[2] so I would have to start telling him about my brother, and he wouldn't even wait till I was finished, would he, the psychiatrist, he'd commit[3] me.

I said that to Mother; she laughed. "You're hard on that boy, Val."

"Boy," I said. "*Man.*"

She laughed, she admitted it. "But remember," she said, "the Lord loves a lunatic."[4]

"How do you know," I said, "seeing you're an atheist?"[5]

Some things he couldn't help.[6] Being born, for instance. He was born the week I started school, and how's that for timing?[7] I was scared, it wasn't like now when the kids have been going to play-school and kindergarten for years. I was going to school for the first time and all the other kids had their mothers with them and where was mine? In the hospital having a baby. The embarrassment to me. There was a lot of shame about those things then.

It wasn't his fault getting born and it wasn't his fault throwing up at my wedding. Think of it. The floor, the table, he even managed to hit the cake. He was not drunk, as some people thought, he really did have some violent kind of flu,[8] which Haro and I came down with,[9] in fact, on our honeymoon. I never heard of anybody else with any kind of flu throwing up over a table with a lace cloth and silver candlesticks and wedding cake on it, but you could say it was bad luck; maybe everybody else when the need came on them was closer to a toilet. And everybody else might try a little harder to hold back,[10] they just might, because nobody else is quite so special,[11] quite so center-of-the-universe, as my baby brother. Just call him a child of nature. That was what he called himself, later on.

I will skip over what he did between getting born and throwing up at my wedding except to say that he had asthma[12] and got to stay home from school weeks on end, listening to soap operas.[13] Sometimes there was a truce[14] between

1 **psychiatrist:** a doctor who treats mental illness
2 **naturally:** (here) of course
3 **commit:** (here) put in a mental institution
4 **the Lord loves a lunatic:** God loves a crazy person
5 **atheist:** person who doesn't believe in God
6 **couldn't help:** (here) couldn't avoid
7 **timing:** (here) scheduling
8 **flu:** influenza (a short-term illness)
9 **came down with:** became sick with
10 **hold back:** hesitate
11 **quite so special:** (here) the narrator is speaking with a sarcastic tone and means the opposite
12 **asthma:** illness with symptoms of severe breathing difficulties
13 **soap operas:** daytime television or radio programs with complicated plots that continue for weeks
14 **truce:** temporary pause in a war

us, and I would get him to tell me what happened every day on "Big Sister" and
30 "Road of Life" and the one with Gee-Gee and Papa David. He was very good at
remembering all the characters and getting all the complications straight, I'll say
that, and he did read a lot in *Gateways to Bookland*, that lovely set Mother bought
for us and that he later sneaked out of the house and sold, for ten dollars, to a
secondhand book dealer.[15] Mother said he could have been brilliant at school if he
wanted to be. That's a deep[16] one, your brother, she used to say, he's got some
surprises in store[17] for us. She was right, he had.

He started staying home permanently in Grade Ten after a little problem[18] of
being caught in a cheating-ring[19] that was getting math tests from some teacher's
desk. One of the janitors[20] was letting him back in the classroom after school
40 because he said he was working on a special project. So he was, in his own way.
Mother said he did it to make himself popular, because he had asthma and
couldn't take part in sports.

Now. Jobs. The question comes up, what is such a person as my brother—and
I ought to give him a name at least, his name is Cam, for Cameron, Mother
thought that would be suitable name for a university president or honest tycoon[21]
(which was the sort of thing she planned for him to be)—what is he going to do,
how is he going to make a living? Until recently the country did not pay you to sit
on your uppers and announce that you had adopted a creative lifestyle. He got a
job first as a movie usher.[22] Mother got it for him, she knew the manager, it was
50 the old International Theater over on Blake Street. He had to quit though, because
he got this darkness-phobia.[23] All the people sitting in the dark he said gave him a
crawly feeling,[24] very peculiar. It only interfered with him working as an usher, it
didn't interfere with him going to the movies on his own.[25] He got very fond of
movies. In fact, he spent whole days sitting in movie houses, sitting through
every show twice then going to another theater and sitting through what was
there. He had to do something with his time, because Mother and all of us
believed he was working then in the office of the Greyhound Bus Depot.[26] He
went off to work at the right time every morning and came home at the right time
every night, and he told all about the cranky[27] old man in charge of the office and
60 the woman with curvature of the spine who had been there since 1919 and how
mad she got at the young girls chewing gum, oh, a lively story, it would have

15 **secondhand book dealer:** someone who
sells used books
16 **deep:** (here) serious
17 **in store:** (here) waiting
18 **a little problem:** (here) the narrator is using
a sarcastic tone and means the opposite
19 **cheating ring:** group of people involved in
cheating
20 **janitors:** people who clean and make
repairs in buildings

21 **tycoon:** wealthy and powerful businessman
22 **usher:** person who shows people where to
sit
23 **darkness-phobia:** fear of darkness
24 **crawly feeling:** feeling of insects crawling
on the skin
25 **on his own:** by himself
26 **bus depot:** bus station
27 **cranky:** irritable

worked up to something as good as the soap operas if Mother hadn't phoned up to complain about the way they were withholding[28] his pay check—due to a technical error in the spelling of his name, he said—and found out he'd quit in the middle of his second day.

Well. Sitting in movies was better than sitting in beer parlors, Mother said. At least he wasn't on the street getting in with criminal gangs. She asked him what his favorite movie was and he said *Seven Brides for Seven Brothers*.[29] See, she said, he is interested in an outdoor life, he is not suited to office work. So she sent him to work for some cousins of hers who have a farm in the Fraser Valley.[30] I **70** should explain that my father, Cam's and mine, was dead by this time, he died away back when Cam was having asthma and listening to soap operas. It didn't make much difference, his dying, because he worked as a conductor on the PGE[31] when it started at Squamish, and he lived part of the time in Lillooet. Nothing changed, Mother went on working at Eaton's[32] as she always had, going across on the ferry[33] and then on the bus; I got supper, she came trudging up the hill in the winter dark.

Cam took off[34] from the farm, he complained that the cousins were religious and always after his soul. Mother could see his problem, she had after all brought him up to be a freethinker. He hitchhiked[35] east. From time to time a letter came. **80** A request for funds.[36] He had been offered a job in northern Quebec[37] if he could get the money together to get up there. Mother sent it. He sent word the job had folded,[38] but he didn't send back the money. He and two friends were going to start a turkey farm. They sent us plans, estimates. They were supposed to be working on contract for the Purina Company, nothing could go wrong. The turkeys were drowned in a flood, after mother had sent him money and we had too against our better judgment.[39] Everywhere that boy hits turns into a disaster area, Mother said. If you read it in a book you wouldn't believe it, she said. It's so terrible it's funny.

She knew. I used to go over to see her on Wednesday afternoon—her day **90** off[40]—pushing the stroller[41] with Karen in it, and later Tommy in it and Karen walking beside, up Lonsdale and down King's Road, and what would we always end up talking about? That boy and I, we are getting a divorce, she said. I am definitely going to write him off.[42] What good will he ever be until he stops

---

28 **withholding:** not sending
29 ***Seven Brides for Seven Brothers*:** movie describing a farming family in the western United States
30 **Fraser Valley:** valley in British Columbia
31 **worked as a conductor on the PGE:** collected passenger tickets on the Pacific Great Eastern railroad in British Columbia
32 **Eaton's:** chain of stores in Canada
33 **ferry:** boat used for transportation, such as to an island
34 **took off:** (here) went away

35 **hitchhiked:** got free rides by standing on the side of the road and sticking his thumb out
36 **funds:** money
37 **Quebec:** province in Canada
38 **folded:** (here) ended
39 **against our better judgment:** even though we knew we shouldn't
40 **day off:** day of rest from work
41 **stroller:** small chair with wheels for very young children
42 **write him off:** consider him a failure

relying on me, she asked. I kept my mouth shut, more or less. She knew my opinion. But she ended up every time saying, "He was a nice fellow to have around the house, though. Good company. That boy could always make me laugh."

Or, "He had a lot to contend with, his asthma and no dad. He never did
100 intentionally hurt a soul."

"One good thing he did," she said, "you could really call it a good turn.[43] That girl."

Referring to the girl who came and told us she had been engaged[44] to him, in Hamilton, Ontario, until he told her he could never get married because he had just found out there was hereditary fatal kidney disease[45] in his family. He wrote her a letter. And she came looking for him to tell him it didn't matter. Not at all a bad-looking girl. She worked for the Bell Telephone. Mother said it was a lie told out of kindness, to spare her feelings when he didn't want to marry her. I said it was a kindness, anyway, because she would have been supporting him for the rest
110 of his life.

Though it might have eased things up a bit on the rest of us.

But that was then and now is now and as we all know times have changed. Cam is finding it easier. He lives at home, off and on,[46] has for a year and a half. His hair is thin in front, not surprising in a man thirty-four years of age, but shoulder-length behind, straggly, graying. He wears a sort of rough brown robe that looks as if it might be made out of a sack[47] (is that what sackcloth[48] is supposed to be, I said to Haro, I wouldn't mind supplying the ashes), and hanging down on his chest he has all sorts of chains, medallions, crosses, elk's teeth or whatnot. Rope sandals on his feet. Some friend of his makes them. He collects
120 welfare.[49] Nobody asks him to work. Who could be so crude? If he has to write down his occupation he writes priest.

It's true. There is a whole school of them, calling themselves priests, and they have a house over in Kitsilano, Cam stays there too sometimes. They're in competition with the Hare Krishna[50] bunch,[51] only these ones don't chant, they just walk around smiling. He has developed this voice I can't stand, a very thin, sweet voice, all on one level. It makes me want to stand in front of him and say, "There's an earthquake in Chile, two hundred thousand people just died, they've burned up another village in Vietnam, famine as usual in India." Just to see if he'd keep saying, "Ve-ery ni-ice, ve-ery ni-ice," that sweet way. He won't eat
130 meat, of course, he eats whole-grain cereals and leafy vegetables. He came into

---

43 good turn: favor
44 engaged: (here) planning to marry
45 fatal kidney disease: kidney disease that will kill him
46 off and on: sometimes
47 sack: bag made of rough material
48 sackcloth: in the Middle Ages, some religious people wore sackcloth and ashes as a form of self-punishment
49 welfare: money from the government because he doesn't have a job
50 Hare Krishna: a religious group
51 bunch: (slang) group of people

the kitchen where I was slicing beets—beets being forbidden, a root vegetable—and, "I hope you understand that you're committing murder," he said.

"No," I said, "but I'll give you sixty seconds to get out of here or I may be."[52]

So as I say he's home part of the time now and he was there on the Monday night when Mother got sick. She was vomiting. A couple of days before this he had started her on a vegetarian[53] diet—she was always promising him she'd try it—and he told her she was vomiting up all the old poisons stored up in her body from eating meat and sugar and so on. He said it was a good sign, and when she had it all vomited out she'd feel better. She kept vomiting, and she didn't feel better, but he had to go out. Monday nights is when they have the weekly meeting 140 at the priests' house, where they chant and burn incense or celebrate the black mass,[54] for all I know.[55] He stayed out most of the night, and when he got home he found Mother unconscious on the bathroom floor. He got on the phone and phoned *me*.

"I think you better come over here and see if you can help Mom, Val."

"What's the matter with her?"

"She's not feeling very well."

"What's the matter with her? Put her on the phone."

"I can't." ·

"Why can't you?" 150

I swear[56] he tittered.[57] "Well I'm afraid she's passed out."[58]

I called the ambulance and sent them for her, that was how she got to the hospital, five o'clock in the morning. I called her family doctor, he got over there, and he got Dr. Ellis Bell, one of the best-known heart men[59] in the city, because that was what they had decided it was, her heart. I got dressed and woke Haro and told him and then I drove myself over to the Lions Gate Hospital. They wouldn't let me in till ten o'clock. They had her in Intensive Care. I sat outside Intensive Care[60] in their slick little awful waiting room. They had red slippery chairs, cheap covering, and a stand full of pebbles with green plastic leaves growing up. I sat there hour after hour and read *The Reader's Digest*.[61] The jokes. Thinking this is 160 how it is, this is it, really, she's dying. Now, this moment, behind those doors, dying. Nothing stops or holds off for it the way you somehow and against all your sense believe it will. I thought about Mother's life, the part of it I knew. Going to work every day, first on the ferry then on the bus. Shopping at the old Red-and-White then at the new Safeway—new, fifteen years old! Going down to the library one night a week, taking me with her, and we would come home on the

---

52 or I may be: (here) or I will be a murderer
53 vegetarian: meatless
54 black mass: religious ritual for the evil force
55 for all I know: this extreme situation could be true (but I don't know)
56 swear: (here) promise it's true
57 tittered: giggled nervously

58 passed out: (slang) unconscious
59 heart men: (slang) doctors who treat heart disease
60 Intensive Care: part of the hospital for the very sick
61 *The Reader's Digest*: magazine that has shortened articles and jokes and is often found in waiting rooms

bus with our load of books and a bag of grapes we bought at the Chinese place, for a treat.[62] Wednesday afternoons too when my kids were small and I went over there to drink coffee and she rolled us cigarettes on that contraption she had. And I thought, all these things don't seem that much like life, when you're doing them, they're just what you do, how you fill up your days, and you think all the time something is going to crack open, and you'll find yourself, *then* you'll find yourself, in life. It's not even that you particularly want this to happen, this cracking open, you're comfortable enough the way things are, but you do expect it. Then you're dying, Mother is dying, and it's just the same plastic chairs and plastic plants and ordinary day outside with people getting groceries and what you've had is all there is, and going to the Library, just a thing like that, coming back up the hill on the bus with books and a bag of grapes seems now worth wanting, O God doesn't it, you'd break your heart[63] wanting back there.

When they let me in to see her she was bluish-gray in the face and her eyes were not all-the-way closed, but they had rolled up, the slit that was open showed the whites. She always looked terrible with her teeth out, anyway, wouldn't let us see her. Cam teased her vanity.[64] They were out now. So all the time, I thought, all the time even when she was young it was in her that she was going to look like this.

They didn't hold out hope. Haro came and took a look at her and put his arm around my shoulders and said, "Val, you'll have to be prepared." He meant well but I couldn't talk to him. It wasn't his mother and he couldn't remember anything. That wasn't his fault but I didn't want to talk to him, I didn't want to listen to him telling me I better be prepared. We went and ate something in the hospital cafeteria.

"You better phone Cam," Haro said.

"Why?"

"He'll want to know."

"Why do you think he'll want to know? He left her alone last night and he didn't know enough to get an ambulance when he came in and found her this morning."

"Just the same. He has a right. Maybe you ought to tell him to get over here."

"He is probably busy this moment preparing to give her a hippie[65] funeral."

But Haro persuaded me as he always can and I went and phoned. No answer. I felt better because I had phoned, and justified in what I had said because of Cam not being in. I went back and waited, by myself.

About seven o'clock that night Cam turned up. He was not alone. He had brought along a tribe of co-priests, I suppose they were, from that house. They all wore the same kind of outfit he did, the brown sacking nightgown and the chains

---

and crosses and holy hardware, they all had long hair, they were all a good many years younger than Cam, except for one old man, really old, with a curly gray beard and bare feet—in March, bare feet—and no teeth. I swear this old man didn't have a clue[66] what was going on. I think they picked him up down by the Salvation Army[67] and put that outfit on him because they needed an old man for a kind of mascot,[68] or extra holiness, or something.   **210**

Cam, said, "This is my sister Valerie. This is Brother Michael. This is Brother John, this is Brother Louis." Etc., etc.

"They haven't said anything to give me hope, Cam. She is dying."

"We hope not," said Cam with his secret smile. "We spent the day working for her."

"Do you mean praying?" I said.

"Work is a better word to describe it than praying, if you don't understand what it is."

Well of course, I never understand.

"Real praying is work, believe me," says Cam and they all smile at me, his **220** way. They can't keep still, like children who have to go to the bathroom they're weaving[69] and jiggling and doing little steps.

"Now where's her room?" says Cam in a practical tone of voice.

I thought of Mother dying and through that slit between her lids—who knows, maybe she can see from time to time—seeing this crowd of dervishes[70] celebrating around her bed. Mother who lost her religion when she was thirteen and went to the Unitarian Church[71] and quit when they had the split[72] about crossing God out of the hymns[73] (she was for it), Mother having to spend her last conscious minutes wondering what had happened, if she was transported back in history to where loonies[74] cavorted around in their crazy ceremonies, trying to **230** sort her last reasonable thoughts out in the middle of their business.

Thank God the nurse said no. The intern[75] was brought and he said no. Cam didn't insist, he smiled and nodded at them as if they were granting permission and then he brought the troupe back into the waiting room and there, right before my eyes, they started. They put the old man in the center, sitting down with his head bowed and his eyes shut—they had to tap him and remind him how to do that—and they squatted[76] in a rough sort of circle round him, facing in and out, in and out, alternately. Then, eyes closed, they started swaying back and forth moaning some words very softly, only not the same words, it sounded as if each

66 didn't have a clue: didn't understand
67 Salvation Army: religious group that provides shelter for poor and homeless people
68 mascot: person or animal used to bring good luck to a group, such as the symbol of a bear for a football team
69 weaving: not walking a straight line
70 dervishes: members of religious groups that dance by turning around in circles

71 Unitarian Church: church with a philosophy of accepting different religious beliefs
72 the split: the division
73 hymns: religious songs
74 loonies: (slang) crazy people
75 intern: (here) young doctor in training
76 squatted: sat on their heels

240 one of them had got different words, and not in English of course but Swahili or Sanskrit or something. It got louder, gradually it got louder, a pounding singsong, and as it did they rose to their feet, all except the old man who stayed where he was and looked as if he might have gone to sleep, sitting, and they began a shuffling[77] kind of dance where they stood, clapping, not very well in time.[78] They did this for a long while, and the noise they were making, though it was not terribly loud, attracted the nurses from their station and nurses' aides and orderlies[79] and a few people like me who were waiting, and nobody seemed to know what to do, because it was so unbelievable, so crazy in that ordinary little waiting room. Everybody just stared as if they were asleep and dreaming and

250 expecting to wake up. Then a nurse came out of Intensive Care and said, "We can't have this disturbance. What do you think you're doing here?"[80]

She took hold of one of the young ones and shook him by the shoulder, else she couldn't have got anybody to stop and pay attention.

"We're working to help a woman who's very sick," he told her.

"I don't know what you call working, but you're not helping anybody. Now I'm asking you to clear out[81] of here. Excuse me.[82] I'm not asking. I'm telling."

"You're very mistaken if you think the tones of our voices are hurting or disturbing any sick person. This whole ceremony is pitched at a level which will reach and comfort the unconscious mind and draw the demonic[83] influences out of

260 the body. It's a ceremony that goes back five thousand years."

"Good Lord,"[84] said the nurse, looking stupefied[85] as well she might.[86] "Who are these people?"

I had to go and enlighten her, telling her that it was my brother and what you might call his friends, and I was not in on[87] their ceremony. I asked about Mother, was there any change.

"No change," she said. "What do we have to do to get them out of here?"

"Turn the hose on them,"[88] one of the orderlies said, and all this time, the dance, or ceremony, never stopped, and the one who had stopped and done the explaining went back to dancing too, and I said to the nurse, "I'll phone in to see

270 how she is, I'm going home for a little while." I walked out of the hospital and found to my surprise that it was dark. The whole day in there, dark to dark. In the parking lot I started to cry. Cam has turned this into a circus for his own benefit, I said to myself, and said it out loud when I got home.

---

77 shuffling: walking without picking up the feet
78 in time: (here) at the same time as the rhythm of the song
79 orderlies: hospital workers who help nurses
80 What do you think you're doing here?: What's the explanation for what you're doing?
81 clear out: get out
82 Excuse me: (here) I made a mistake and should have said *telling,* not *asking*
83 demonic: evil
84 Good Lord: exclamation of surprise or shock
85 stupefied: amazed; astonished
86 as well she might: as she had good reason to do
87 not in on: not part of
88 turn the hose on them: turn the force of the water from the hose on them

Haro made me a drink.

"It'll probably get into the papers,"[89] I said. "Cam's chance for fame."

Haro phoned the hospital to see if there was any news and they said there wasn't. "Did they have—was there any difficulty with some young people in the waiting room this evening? Did they leave quietly?" Haro is ten years older than I am, a cautious man, too patient with everybody. I used to think he was sometimes giving Cam money I didn't know about. **280**

"They left quietly," he said. "Don't worry about the papers. Get some sleep."

I didn't mean to but I fell asleep on the couch, after the drink and the long day. I woke up with the phone ringing and day lightening the room. I stumbled into the kitchen dragging the blanket Haro had put over me and saw by the clock on the wall it was a quarter to six. She's gone, I thought.

It was her own doctor.

He said he had encouraging news. He said she was much better this morning.

I dragged over a chair and collapsed[90] in it, both arms and my head too down on the kitchen counter. I came back on the phone to hear him saying she was still in a critical[91] phase and the next forty-eight hours would tell the story, but without **290** raising my hopes too high he wanted me to know she was responding to treatment. He said that this was especially surprising in view of the fact that she had been late getting to hospital and the things they did to her at first did not seem to have much effect, though of course the fact that she survived the first few hours at all was a good sign.[92] Nobody had made much of this good sign to me yesterday, I thought.

I sat there for an hour at least after I had hung up the phone. I made a cup of instant coffee and my hands were shaking so I could hardly get the water into the cup, then couldn't get the cup to my mouth. I let it go cold. Haro came out in his pyjamas at last. He gave me one look and said, "Easy, Val. Has she gone?" **300**

"She's some better. She's responding to treatment."

"The look of you I thought the other."[93]

"I'm so amazed."

"I wouldn't've given five cents for her chances yesterday noon."

"I know. I can't believe it."

"It's the tension," Haro said. "I know. You build yourself up ready for something bad to happen and then when it doesn't, it's a queer feeling, you can't feel good right away, it's almost like a disappointment."

Disappointment. That was the word that stayed with me. I was so glad, really, grateful, but underneath I was thinking, so Cam didn't kill her after all, with his **310** carelessness and craziness and going out and neglecting[94] her he didn't kill her,

---

89 papers: newspapers
90 collapsed: fell down because of exhaustion, weakness, or emotional upset
91 critical: serious
92 good sign: indication that the future will be good
93 I thought the other: I thought the other possibility (that is, I thought she had died)
94 neglecting: not taking care of

and I was, yes, I was, sorry in some part of me to find out that was true. And I knew Haro knew this but wouldn't speak of it to me, ever. That was the real shock to me, why I kept shaking. Not whether Mother lived or died. It was what was so plain about myself.

Mother got well, she pulled through[95] beautifully. After she rallied she never sank back. She was in the hospital three weeks and then she came home, and rested another three weeks, and after that went back to work, cutting down a bit and working ten to four[96] instead of full days, what they call the housewives'
320   shift. She told everybody about Cam and his friends coming to the hospital. She began to say things like, "Well, that boy of mine may not be much of a success at anything else but you have to admit he has a knack[97] of saving lives." Or, "Maybe Cam should go into the miracle[98] business, he certainly pulled it off with me." By this time Cam was saying, he is saying now, that he's not sure about that religion, he's getting tired of the other priests and all that not eating meat or root vegetables. It's a stage,[99] he says now, he's glad he went through it, self-discovery. One day I went over there and found he was trying on an old suit and tie. He says he might take advantage of some of the adult education courses, he is thinking of becoming an accountant.[100]
330   I was thinking myself about changing into a different sort of person from the one I am. I do think about that. I read a book called *The Art of Loving*. A lot of things seemed clear while I was reading it but afterwards I went back to being more or less the same. What has Cam ever done that actually hurt me, anyway, as Haro once said. And how am I better than he is after the way I felt the night Mother lived instead of died? I made a promise to myself I would try. I went over there one day taking them a bakery cake—which Cam eats now as happily as anybody else—and I heard their voices out in the yard—now it's summer, they love to sit in the sun—Mother saying to some visitor, "Oh yes I was, I was all set to take off into the wild blue yonder, and Cam here, this *idiot*, came and danced
340   outside my door with a bunch of his hippie friends—"

"My God, woman," roared Cam, but you could tell he didn't care now, "members of an ancient holy discipline."

I had a strange feeling, like I was walking on coals[101] and trying a spell so I wouldn't get burnt.

Forgiveness in families is a mystery to me, how it comes or how it lasts.

---

95 pulled through: survived
96 ten to four: from 10:00 in the morning to 4:00 in the afternoon
97 knack: skill
98 miracle: something wonderful that can't be explained by the laws of nature and so is thought to be an act of God

99 stage: (here) period in which a person's character changes
100 accountant: person who takes care of a company's financial records
101 walking on coals: walking on hot coals, as some members of a religious group in India can do without burning their feet

Understanding the Story

Work individually or with another student to answer these comprehension questions and review the story's events.

Mark each of the following sentences true or false. If it's true, explain further. If it's false, correct the sentence.

1.___ The narrator's brother, Cam, threw up at the narrator's wedding.

2.___ The narrator, Val, and her husband, Haro, had the flu on their honeymoon.

3.___ Cam had asthma as a child and stayed home from school, playing chess.

Finish these sentences:

4. a) Cam read a lot in "Gateways to Bookland," but then he

_____.

(What did his mother say about this?)

b) In school, Cam was caught _____.

(What did his mother say about this?)

5. Describe what happened when Cam had a job as a movie usher. Why did he quit? What did he do then? How did his family find out he'd quit?

6. Where did Cam's father work before he died? Where does Cam's mother work?

7. What happened when Cam went to live on a farm? Describe what he did next.

8. Retell the story by filling in the blanks in the following sentences:

a) After Cam joined the religious group, he began to wear _____. He wouldn't eat _____ or _____ and he lived with _____.

b) One Monday night, Cam's mother wasn't feeling well; she kept

_____. Cam went out to a meeting of his religious group. When he got home, _____. Cam called his sister and said _____.

c) Val called_____ and then she went to the _____. Her husband wanted her to be prepared for _____.

d) Cam arrived with _____. In the waiting room, they _____.

Mark each sentence true or false. If it's true, explain further. If it's false, correct the sentence.

9.____ The nurses and other employees of the hospital enjoyed watching Cam and his friends.

10.____ After Val went home, she fell asleep. When the phone rang, it was her mother's doctor with good news.

11.____ The mother's health got better.

12.____ Cam is still with the religious group.

Talking and Writing

With your classmates, use these questions as starting points for a discussion of ideas presented in the story. Then select a question and write an essay on the topic.

1. What kind of a person was Cam? What did Cam do that annoyed his sister, the narrator of the story? Did he irritate other people as well? What was funny about him?

For example, what was irritating or funny about:
- his selling the family book *Gateways to Bookland*
- his stealing math tests
- his job experience as a movie usher
- his plans to make money on a turkey farm
- his actions the night Mother was sick
- his visit to the hospital

2. What do you think will happen to Cam? Can he change?

If Cam becomes an accountant, would you want him to prepare your tax forms? Would you like to be his boss? What would it be like to work for Cam?

3. Do you think Val is too severe with Cam, or the mother is too forgiving? Why do you think Val and the mother react differently to Cam? (Why doesn't Val just ignore Cam?)

How would you describe the relationship between Cam and his mother? Between Cam and his sister?

4. What did Cam do for his mother? Did he help her or hurt her?

5. What did Val think about while she was sitting in the waiting room in the hospital? How does she feel about her experiences in life, looking back?

6. What does the narrator mean by the last line of the story? Why does she feel differently now about Cam and about herself?

7. Why was it difficult for Val to talk with her husband, Haro, while her mother was sick?

More Ideas

1. Other books by Alice Munro include *Dance of the Happy Shades* and *The Beggar Maid.*

Suggested reading by Canadian English-speaking writers: *A Bird in the House* and *A Jest of God* by Margaret Laurence; *Cat's Eye* and *Dancing Girls* by Margaret Atwood; *In the Skin of the Lion* by Michael Ondaatje; *Stones* and *The Wars* by Timothy Findley; *Shoeless Joe* by W. P. Kinsella; *Digging Up the Mountains* by Neil Bissoondath; and *Home Truths* by Mavis Gallant.

Collections of Canadian short stories include *The Penguin Book of Modern Canadian Short Stories*, edited by Wayne Grady; *Best Canadian Short Stores*, edited by John Stevens; and *Great Canadian Short Stories*, selected by Alec Lucas.

2. Find out about British Columbia, where this story takes place. For example, what do Vancouver and Vancouver Island look like? What are the Rocky Mountains (the Rockies)? If you can find photos in books, bring them to class.

You could find out about some of the people of British Columbia. For example, where do the Haida Indians live? What is unusual about their art? (What's a totem pole? A canoe?)

Or you could find out about the history of British Columbia. For example, what happened when gold was discovered in 1858?

3. Write a short paper about someone you know (or someone you've heard of) who drives other people crazy. How do other people react to this person's behavior?

   Or you could describe a specific event that was particularly irritating. (Governmental agencies can be a good source of irritating people.) What's the best way to handle these frustrating experiences?

4. Try writing a letter of complaint or role-playing in class. For example: You ordered a box of dishes but instead you received a box of baby diapers. Or your bank keeps taking money out of your bank account every time you make a deposit.

   Or the telephone company is charging you for making calls to people you don't know who live thousands of miles away. Or the first time you washed a new shirt, it became four sizes smaller.

Building Vocabulary

1. In casual, spoken English, we use many incomplete and run-on sentences to communicate. In this story, the author sometimes chooses to write very short or very long sentences.

   Try rewriting a few sentences from this story in a more formal written style. For example, try rewriting the first paragraph (or parts of the sixth or seventh paragraphs) at the beginning of the story. Or try rewriting parts of the long paragraph on page 139.

   How does this editing affect the flow of the writing? How does the rewriting change the mood?

2. Complete each of the following sentences, using the appropriate words from this list. Be sure to use the correct form of each word.

atheism	psychiatry	day off
accounting	flu	asthmatic
good turn	off and on	crankiness
secondhand	good sign	miraculous
neglected	collapsing	ferry

   a) To encourage people to help each other, we have a saying: "One

   _____ deserves another."

   b) An _____ has to be very precise with numbers.

c) An _____ isn't a member of a religion.

d) When people have _____, they sometimes can't breathe very well.

e) I've been studying English _____ for many years.

f) If a student doesn't do well in high school, many people think it's not a _____ that he or she will do well in college.

g) You can save a lot of money by buying furniture _____.

h) Sometimes people who are unhappy talk to a _____.

i) When the weather's cold in the winter, a lot of people have the _____ for a few days or longer.

j) On our vacation, we're taking the _____ from Maine to Nova Scotia.

k) When you own your own business, it's hard to take a _____.

l) The baby was so _____ we put her to bed.

m) Val was afraid that her mother would die because of Cam's _____.

n) Val's mother was sure her recovery was a _____.

o) I was so tired last night that I _____ as soon as I got home.